To Pq

"The Rose of the Well, abin to the real anyway! thru Jesus our Saviour!

GOD BLESS YOU ALWAYS

Ann Wiley Evans
Eph 3:20

HOLD ON TO YOUR FORK

By

John Wiley Evans

©2011, John W. Evans. All rights reserved.

Edited and formatted by Jon Evans and Jim Evans.
Cover art by Jim Evans.

Preface

It is with real joy in Christ that I herein submit my second book of original poems and songs for the public's approval and usefulness. Since my birth in the year 1928 in Oklahoma, and my receiving Christ as my Savior in the year 1940, it has been a God-blest journey for me—not without sins and mistakes aplenty along the way, of course, which my God has overruled, forgiving me graciously. During those many years I served a stint with the U.S. Marines, and graduated from three institutions of higher learning: Bob Jones University, Grace Theological Seminary, and Indiana University. Over a period of thirty-five years, I pastored eight churches: first in Dayton, Ohio; then, in Indiana: in Sidney, Flora, Peru, Bloomfield, Perrysburg, and two in the Royal Center area. I taught public school for thirty-three years also; but it was not until after I had retired from my pastoral ministries and public school teaching that I began writing poetry and songs, getting my first book published in 2004.

I want especially to express a deep appreciation to Joyce Runyon Evans, my beloved wife of 59 years, for all she has meant to me and my ministries through the years. She has been my pianist since we married in 1952 (At college, I "advertised" for a wife who could play the piano and could make a good cup of coffee!). We have been conducting services each month in several nursing homes since moving to Florida in 1993, and with her piano playing she has blessed many an oldster. Joyce also continues to be an integral part of my Sunday-school ministry with the Jacksonville First Baptist Church. And, of course, Joyce also has given me four wonderful children, all active Christians who love Jesus: Jonathan, Jeffrey, James, and Joy; they have contributed much to my overall ministry—and have given me eleven wonderful grandchildren.

Incidentally, "Hold Onto Your Fork," the poem around which I am privileged to make these presentations today, is found on page 140. It is a tribute to my mother, who also deserves much credit for anything worthwhile one can find in my efforts in these writings. She reared me primarily to serve my God; I gratefully give credit here. May God rest her soul there in glory!

Finally, I commit my efforts to you my readers. I pray God may use these humble efforts somehow to win hearts to Himself, that I shall see some in glory some day who may tell me that they found the Savior through these poems and songs. Certainly the "Giver of every perfect gift" deserves all my praise; and I readily say everything I am or hope to be I owe to Him. Praise Him evermore with me!

– John Wiley Evans, Spring 2011

Hold On to Your Fork
By John Wiley Evans

Table of Contents

PREFACE I
CHAPTER ONE: POEMS ON CHRISTMAS AND CHRIST 1
   'TWAS CHRISTMAS EVE IN WORLD WAR ONE 2
   BUTTERFLY, DO FLUTTER BY 3
   HELP US, LORD, AT CHRISTMASTIME 4
   LIGHT FROM OUR CHRISTMAS TREE 5
   ON BEING "SALT" AT CHRISTMAS 6
   "I'LL JUST TOUCH HIS GARMENT" 7
   HOW STRANGE IT ALL SEEMS! 8
   A POET'S TWENTY-THIRD PSALM 9
   "MY GOD, WHY HAVE YOU FORSAKEN ME?" 10
   GETHSEMANE, GABBATHA, GOLGOTHA! 10
   OUR LORD ONCE APPEARED IN IRAQ 11
   CHRIST'S CROSS, SHEPHERD'S CROOK, AND HIS CROWN 11
   THAT OTHER "WOMAN AT THE WELL" 12
   CHRIST DINES WITH TRUSTING HEARTS 12
   "THE PASSION OF THE CHRIST" AND PAIN 13
   "A WORD TO THE WISE" 14
   LOVE'S WRITTEN IN HIS HANDS! 14
   JEHOVAH-JIREH—JESUS-PROVIDER 16
   IS JESUS AS "SON" TRULY GOD? 17
   CHRIST'S VIRGIN BIRTH 18
   O BLEST HEAVEN'S VISION! 19
   JESUS IS OUR "AMEN" 20
   CHRIST IS OUR ALL IN ALL, EVEN "HOME" 20
   DELIVERANCE: PAST, PRESENT, AND FUTURE 21
   GOT JESUS? 22
   CHRIST IS JEHOVAH GOD! 23
   OH THE BLOOD OF JESUS! 24
   BUDDY 25
   THIS BRIDGE WON'T LET YOU DOWN 27
   THE MOST BEAUTIFUL TREE AT CHRISTMAS 28

CHAPTER TWO: POEMS ON GOD'S "SO GREAT SALVATION" 29
   ON JUNE THE NINTH IN 1940 30
   PROVIDENCE, PREDESTINATION, AND FREE WILL 31

Title	Page
Real Hope and Timeless Happiness	32
Good Works and Man's Salvation	33
If You Should Die Tonight	34
Just One, Lest Presuming Men Rue	35
Five Brides of Genesis and Christ's Church	36
The Triune God in My Salvation	36
Faith and Works Are Wed	37
There's No Assessing of "Double Jeopardy!"	37
Gleaning for Life's Meaning	38
A Dinnertime Tale	39
"None of Ours Is Lost!"	41
God's Elect and Me	41
"Lord, This Is What You Said"	42
Two Webs Woven	43
"Up" or "Down"?	44
My Faith this July Fourth	45
"The Impossible" Is Still Possible!	47
God's Great Invitation to "Come!"	47
"All Things Are Yours!"	48
The "Exceeding Abundantly Able" God	48
"Tsunamis" Break Deep from the Breast	50
God's Zeal	51
There's Power with God in an "If"	52
Mephibosheth Was Like Ourselves	53
An Empty Eggshell	54
God, Too, Worked at that Scene!	56
Just Where on "Resurrection" Are You?	57
Of Us and Them	58
Hey, I'm a "Whosoever!"	59
Hey, Who's Holding Whom?	59
Our Saddest War Had Ended	60
A Kiss Can Be a Door	62
On Rushing to Judgment	62
In Wrath, Lord, Remember Your Mercy	64
Am I "A Pancake Half-Baked"?	65
I Know that I by Grace Shall Make It!	66
Caregivers and "Our Good Samaritan"	66
His "Home Sweet Home"	67
Gideon's Success and Sorrow	67
The Christian's Seven-Ups	69
"How Could You Ever Hate Me So?!"	70
I Think That I Shall Never See	71
God's Gifts Given in John 3:16	71
An Addition to His "Home"	73
God's Crazy 'Bout You!	73

My Christian Heart Is a Garden for Christ	74
No "Double Jeopardy"	74
The Ruptured Reed and Smoking Flax	75
The "House" Known as Man	75
"Our God Is In the Gale!"	76
"Sahara-like" We Need Renewal	77
Since Escaping I Would Flee!	78
I Do Desire Your Fullness, Lord!	79
Against Those Savage Situations	79
On Burying Grudges—Not Bearing Them	80
God, Give Us Your Enough!	81
There's a Difference	81
An Example in Candy our Cat	82
He Said "We Shall Go Over"	82
Thus Far the Lord Has Helped Us	83
Hey, I'm Loaded on John 3:16!	84

CHAPTER THREE: POEMS ON THE TONGUE, PRAYER AND PRAISE 87

I'll Praise My God Forever	88
Praise The Son Light! Praise Our God!	89
Praise Is the Primer for Prayer	90
Perfected Praise	90
My Prayer	91
I Pray for Grace Again	91
The Way Is Raised!	92
Prayer Principles	92
Thank God for Prayers Unanswered!	93
Hurricane Katrina and Hope through Prayer	94
November Reflections	95
"He Prays the Best Who loves the Best"	95
On "Hanging Harps on Willow Trees"	97
Our Lord Once Worked a Work for Men	97
That Boneless Tongue!	98
On "Laying Isaac Down"	98
God's Lessons in the Bees	99
Let's Bloom Where We've Been Planted	101
The Night-blooming Cereus	102

CHAPTER FOUR: POEMS RELATED TO PROPHECY, ESPECIALLY TO THE CHURCH AND NATION OF ISRAEL. 103

"The Rapture" in "The Revelation"	104
Just Where Are We in Prophecy?	105
A Lesson from "Hurricane Charley"	107
When "Swords to Ploughshares" Come to Be	108

ISRAEL IN THE CROSS HAIRS	109
GOD'S PROVEN PROVIDENCES	110
DREAD ARMAGEDDON LOOMS!	111
JOSEPH IN PROPHETIC FOCUS	112
THE SAGA OF ISRAEL, THRICE-BORN NOW TO BE	113
MY HOPE FOR ISRAEL'S FUTURE	114
SOME ASK, "IS THIS TO BE....?"	115
THE MESSAGE TO US IN KATRINA	115
WHEN THE TOWERS FELL	116
TILL "COME, FLY AWAY, MY LOVE!"	117
ARISE, O ISRAEL, AND QUIT YOUR QUAKING!	117
PRAY FOR JERUSALEM'S PEACE	118
CHRIST'S SECOND COMING	119
AT LENGTH "THE PAINT MUST DRY!"	120

CHAPTER FIVE: "A LITTLE HUMOR NOW AND THEN" 121

THANKS FOR GOD'S GOOD HUMOR	122
ON SECOND THOUGHT....!	122
SOME POETIC CHURCH BLOOPERS	123
HOW ABOUT THESE "BURMA SHAVE SIGNS"?	123
ODE ON THE EXISTENCE OF LICE FROM EARLIEST TIMES TILL NOW	125
PETS AND "THAT BAD HAIR DAY"	125
A SATURDAY MORNING'S MUTTERING	126
WATCH OUT FOR THOSE FRUIT PEELS!	127
CONFESSION OF A "CRACKED POT"	127
OH HOW GREAT IS THE POTTER WHO REFASHIONED ME!	128
JIM ONCE SAID	128
AT BAT WITH "SAINTS ALIVE"	128
GOD'S GIFT IN MARMALADE	129
THE HOLIDAY FOR ATHEISTS	130
GOD'S RECALL OF HUMANS HERE READ	131
SOME COULD-BE AND WOULD-BE EPITAPHS	132
FOR THAT "GIFT OF CRITICISM"	133
LET'S BE POSITIVE, MY FRIENDS!	134

CHAPTER SIX: POEMS DEDICATED IN MEMORY OF CHERISHED FAMILY AND FRIENDS 135

LIFE HAS TOLD WE ARE OLD, YELLOWED, SERE, DARLING	136
IF I COULD SEIZE A SUNBEAM	136
"JOYCE, M.R.S.!"	137
A QUESTION RESOLVED	137
"GRAMPA, WHAT DO WE KNOW ABOUT HEAVEN....?"	137
FRIENDS ARE FRIENDS FOREVER	138
MY JOYCE	139

"Hold Onto Your Fork!" 140
Together Again 141

CHAPTER SEVEN: "GOD'S BEST IS YET TO BE"—WE'VE HEAVEN TO COME! 143

"God's Best Is Yet To Be!" 144
When Born Men Here Are Seen To Be 145
When "The Shadows Flee Away" 145
How Big We'll Win When We Shall Die! 146
Like Noah's Dove I've Found No Ease 147
Enraptured at Death 149
When "Down Time's" Mine at Last 149
My Epitaph 149

CHAPTER EIGHT: SOME ORIGINAL SONGS GOD HAS GIVEN ME 151

Christmas Means 'Welcome Home!' 138
Jesus Walked My Calvary Road 140
He Chose My Cross, Not His Crown 143
That Old Romans Road 145
From that 'Hole' Up to Heaven 147
Thank God the Garbage is Gone 149
What a Day! 151
You're Worth a World of Little Sparrows 154
Deeper, Let's Go Deeper 156
God's Lamb as Lion King Shall Reign! 158
My Hallelujah Home 161
Released with Great Joy I'll Go Home 164

CHAPTER ONE: POEMS ON CHRISTMAS AND CHRIST

I think it appropriate to begin my latest collection of poems the Lord has given me with those relating to Christmas and Christ, since at Bethlehem it all began in the annals of the greatest Man who ever walked this earth. Certainly I would say, as did former President George W. Bush, that the Christ of Bible fame has had the greatest influence in my life for good. But isn't it amazing that this One, the One Who is to reign forever as King of Kings and Lord of Lords, should be born in a lowly shed for barnyard animals in that long ago? No doubt this humble birth signifies how we too must be born again, spiritually in our case, if we are to make a mark at all in our world for Him. I surely want to be that humble servant, don't you?

This first section of my anthology features "'Twas Christmas Eve in No-man's-Land," a poem centering in the First World War in Europe with our American armed forces there, but I have also included here many others of a diverse nature, several even on the controversy of His virgin birth (no controversy with me!). Also, to bring the Greatest Man Who Ever Lived into a modern-day context, I have included "Jesus Christ Once Appeared in Iraq." I hope my readers enjoy this wide portrayal with the greatest love and honor going to Him. He certainly is "The Greatest" with me!

Yes, I hope and pray that the following efforts will glorify my Lord Jesus Christ of Bethlehem fame. Certainly He has brought fulfillment to me through my some eighty plus years as His servant upon the planet that He created. God grant this continues herein, and I pray this prayer in His Name.

'Twas Christmas Eve in World War One

'Twas Christmas Eve in World War One
When enemies entrenched did wait
On either side of no-man's-land
With hearts befouled by hate.

One wonders how it thus could be,
That horrid war would thus prevail
'Midst nations where in better times
The Prince of Peace they'd hailed.

But such it was. The blood and gall
Of malice now none seemed to quell.
The prophets preaching peace accords
Had now their message—Hell!

Then as it was in normal times
Where harmony long since had been,
A carol rose 'cross no-man's-land
To move the hearts of men.

"Silent night, holy night,
All is calm, all is bright,
'Round yon Virgin, Mother and Child,
Holy Infant so tender and mild.
Sleep in heavenly peace.
Sleep in heavenly peace."

Yes, one lone tenor (who knows who)
In courage lifted high this song,
And soon both sides—now comrades all—
Joined in, their deepest hatred gone!

Those prayerful men, all blending in,
Sang lustily from sorrowed souls.
They must have dreamed they'd void the night,
Their broken world make whole

It would have been a great, great thing
If all ill will that night had ceased;
But dawn, unerring, told the truth—
Hell's demons still hate peace!

And yet it's true one glorious day
That Blessed Babe of Song shall reign;
A thousand years shall know His peace—
And Paradise regained!

Butterfly, Do Flutter By

Butterfly, do flutter by!
How breathlessly you typify
The One Whom prophets prophesy
And angels laud at Christmastide!
Butterfly, O Butterfly!

Butterfly, do flutter by!
We know your colors signify
Him Whom the Magi certified
And brought rich gifts to glorify—
Yes, Christ Born King now, Butterfly!
Butterfly, O Butterfly!

Butterfly, do flutter by!
O praise our Lord once crucified!
Bless His Name and magnify
Him Whom destruction has denied,
Butterfly, O Butterfly!

Butterfly, do flutter by!
See Christ now risen, sanctified!
None up in Heaven would decry
Our God enthroned to vilify—
Laud Him with me, Butterfly!
Butterfly, O Butterfly!

Help Us, Lord, at Christmastime

At Christmastime let's grow in grace;
Let spirits be unbound.
For souls unsaved still watch us here,
Clust'ring all around!

A fault for sure we should disdain
Is lack of FAITH* it's true.
But, God, give more at Christmastime;
We pray such may ensue.

Sometimes we who are prone to pray
In trials fail to cope;
So it's our prayer at Christmastime:
Lord, build our store of HOPE!**

We sadly see at Christmastime
In error some hate life;
And saints sometimes too lack in love—
O God, our LOVE***incite!

A joyfulness at Christmastime
Will give You, Lord, renown.
Erase then sadness that detracts.
May JOY****our faces crown!

Our God's commands at Christmastime
We know come with His GRACE,*****
So help us, Lord, at Christmastime
That such we will embrace!

*Have faith in God."—Mark 11:22;
**Hope thou in God."—Psalm 42:11;
***Let us love one another, for love is of God."—1 John 4:7;
****Rejoice in the Lord always, and again I say, Rejoice."—Phil. 4:4;
*****The Grace of our Lord Jesus Christ be with you."—Romans 16:20.

Light from Our Christmas Tree

At Christmastime with all its cheer
How good it is to see
A symbol of the Gospel near
In our bright Christmas tree!

Its ever-greenness here recalls
Our Lord as ever God.
Longevity in others palls—
Christ only merits laud!

The beauty of the tree suggests
The glory in Christ known,
Which "vying gods" do not possess,
Their darkness surely shown!

And see the lights upon our tree,
Which shed their brightness 'round?
And does not Christ, for all to see,
Light up this world around?

Atop our tree a brilliant star
Shines forth as in the night,
Like one led magi from afar
To Christ Who is "The Light."

You'll also see a central stem
Points upward to the sky,
Where note toward New Jerusalem
Saints move, their spirits high.

At its broad base the limbs enclose
Gifts marvelous in scope,
Reminding us how Christ's love goes
'Round all, inspiring hope.

We're also gifts our Savior gives
To all for men to see,
As God gave Christ, who died yet lives
For all eternally!

"Thanks be unto God for His Unspeakable Gift!"—2 Cor. 9::15.

On Being "Salt" at Christmas
"Ye are the salt of the earth." – Christ, Matt. 5:3

Our table salt's so good – amazing! –
Which we hold in our hands.
Components, too, a lesson give us,
Which now our thoughts command.

For instance, chloride acid's there;
Unmixed it's poison, friend!
But when with sodium we blend it,
Our salt then blesses men!

And note a valid commentary
As to salt's worthwhileness:
From French it comes akin to labor—
Our "SALary," no less!

And, yes, salt has its application
To Christian teachings too.
A madman is in Scripture noted
As dire "chloride" endued!*

But when as "Sodium" our Savior
Came and the man was changed—
Lo, then the Gadarene, now blessing,
A saint God's love proclaimed!

Lord, help me be like that blest man
This Christmas in my place.
Help me as "salt" to go midst "madmen"
To magnify Your grace!
*Mark 5: 1-20

"I'll Just Touch His Garment"
Matthew 9:18-26

The dear woman lacked knowledge of Jesus,
Since details of His person were poor.
If she'd known, she'd not come "like a sneak thief,"
But instead "with a knock at the door."

But she thought, "He'd not want that I face Him,
Since I'm barred by the laws of this day.*
I'll but touch just the hem of His garment,
And with that hope I'm healed—this I pray!"
So she touched Him with crowds pressing on them—
And so quickly she knew she was well!
But our Lord, feeling power go from Him,
Asked, "Who was it who touched me, please tell?"

Then the woman, now healed but so fearful—
Yet so blessed!—did confess it was she;
At which Jesus commended her faith,
And confirmed from her plague she was free.

Now this story most surely speaks to us
Of our Lord's tender mercy and grace—
Even more of His marvelous power,
To heal so in so daunting a case.**

*Leviticus 15:1ff;
**Ephesians 3:20—"God is able to do far more than we would ever dare to ask or even dream of—infinitely beyond our highest prayers, desires, thoughts, or hopes."

How Strange It All Seems!

How strange, as seers said,
In Jews' Bethlehem shed
On that day in the long, long ago,
The Great Savior was born,
As His mother was scorned.
They don't spare her a room, facts will show!

How strange, I conclude,
In that shed, lowly, rude,
Came the good "Bread of Life" in God's love,
Which men lacking must die—
But men won't satisfy
Their dire need with The Best from above!

How strange to this day
That One came as "The Way,"
Thus to guide men to God in this world—
But these balk and won't go
In "The Way" wise men know,
But continue in paths so imperiled!

How strange from my youth
That One known as "The Truth"
Would be born here to give men God's light—
But they choose the big lie
That caused forebears to die,
Thus ignoring their desperate plight!

How strange in man's strife
That He Who is "The Life"
Would for men on a cross that life give—
But they go on in death,
Then will breathe their last breath
Rather than with their Lord ever live!

How strange it all seems!

A Poet's Twenty-third Psalm

The Lord is my Shepherd, in union so grand,
Which means in this life He meets all its demands.
No, there's never occasion for any great want,
With Christ as my Shepherd, my Life-giving Font.

My soul it finds rest in His pastures so green.
He supplies ev'ry need such as none has e'er seen.
Beside the still waters He leads me in peace,
My spirit so quiet, where all fears have ceased.

Remission for sins He gives, and I'm restored;
With healing so precious, I praise Him Adored.
He leads me along His high holy paths.
O my soul so responds in those ways I am cast!

He leads me in righteousness; good deeds are done,
As praises forever ascend to the Son.
And though I may even through death's valley go,
It is but a shadow of itself, I know.

His rod and His staff make for training I need.
These then are my help as for guidance I plead.
He makes me triumph in the enemy's land,
Providing great repasts by His gracious hand.

My head is perfumed by blest oil as from You,
A seal of all blessings by which I'm endued.
So it is by Your grace that my cup overflows.
How great is My Shepherd, this sheep surely knows!

Undeserving through life I go and O so blest,
For indeed You're my Shepherd, translating in rest.
O goodness and mercy pursue me always,
And forever I'll dwell in Your House to Your praise!

"My God, Why Have You Forsaken Me?"
Matt. 27:46; Deut. 21:23; Gal. 3:13

We've heard men say in earthly unbelief
That Christ was victim of a mental loss
In thinking that with God was no relief—
"Indeed, Christ was NOT cast off on the Cross!"

But did our Lord, omniscient as to truth,
E'er have a moment when He did not grasp
The will of God, though other mortals, duped,
Just THINK themselves forsaken in fate cast?

Oh no! Christ knew—He ratified the plan
That said He must "the winepress tread alone,"
"Upon a tree" be cursed as sin's sad LAMB—
So here by blood see human sins atoned!

Praise God Christ Knew, was knowing till the end.
Yes, ALL ALONE THERE JESUS BORE OUR SIN!

Gethsemane, Gabbatha, Golgotha!
Inspired by the movie, "The Passion of Christ"

Gethsemane, Gabbatha, Golgotha!
Where indeed Hell was paid no mind!
Gethsemane, Gabbatha, Golgotha!
Where Love won out for all mankind!
True Christ had heard dread Satan's lies;
Well might these be The Liar's greatest prize!
But, no, with face set as a flint,
His heart set too, valor unspent,
He followed where God's will would go -
And so we're saved, the sequel know!
Gethsemane, Gabbatha, Golgotha!
Where indeed Hell was paid no mind!
Gethsemane, Gabbatha, Golgotha!
Where Love won out for all mankind!

Our Lord Once Appeared in Iraq
Daniel 3

Jesus Christ once appeared in Iraq
To bring cheer to three men far from home.
It was there in a furnace so hot
He brought pow'r, peace and joy never known.

And it's true, as our Bible has taught,
That today many folk "far from home"
In their own "private furnaces hot"
Still have need of this Lord as their own!

I rejoice that it was in Iraq
Where our Lord in His power was known—
But the Same Lord awaits in more scenes quite as hot
There again to appear for His own!

Christ's Cross, Shepherd's Crook, and His Crown
Psalm 22, 23, and 24

To appreciate texts that are given of God,
Do read well there the contexts, my friend.
You will find in so doing your spirit is awed,
And Your soul better fed in the end!

O we know our great psalm, twenty-three, reveals Christ,
Yet there not His full glory we see.
We must look both before and behind—pay that price—
Then more wonderful He comes to be.

Yes, the Savior thrice seen in the psalms we behold:
Twenty-two, on the cross for our sins;
Twenty-three, in the now, as our Shepherd of old;
Twenty-four, as our King in the end.

O yes, friends, let's enjoy twenty-three more each day,
Seeing Christ loving us in renown;
But let's view Him also with all three psalms in play:
With His cross, Shepherd's crook, and His crown.

That Other "Woman at the Well"
Genesis 16:5-14

"The woman at the well" of old gave us as Christians much
To help us live for God as told in Sunday school and such.
And yet a maid, not as well known, named Hagar, Sarai's slave,
Excluded from her home, beside a well was also saved.

Indeed, comparisons I'd chart, and in the naming praise
Our Savior, Christ—ever "The same!"—Who always such souls saved.
Like Sychar's "woman at the well," from social scenes outcast,
This other maid would surely tell of ill-will on her cast.

But some say, "It's an angel we see save her on this scene."
But she said, "Thou God seest me!"—no proxy in between!
Yes, Christ indeed heard prayers made by Hagar, assert—
As said before, in ev'ry age He's saved sad souls that hurt.

And when the maid to Christ had said, "I'm lost so badly here!"
I'd say forgiveness too was pled: Hers was a sinner's prayer.
Just so I'd say the maid was saved assuredly in soul,
For by the word of God obeyed she showed she was made whole.

O as much later Christ gave "drink more sweet than words could tell,"
So Hagar, too, I truly think, drank too from Jesus' well.

Christ Dines with Trusting Hearts

Jerusalem was crowded
With festive folk this day.
Not many minds were clouded
With cares to mar their stay.

The most with their attainments
Had come to feast with friends,
But Christ in God's arrangement
Had come for pain, men's sins.

Yes, some like raging beasts
Were lusting for His blood.
Their hate on Him would feed,
God's way misunderstood.

Aware of men's intentions,
One gave an "upper room,"
Where we've illumination
Of light to bar our gloom:

Our Lord once here with worldlings
Was granted NOT ONE PART,
But then—as NOW with friends—
HE DINES WITH TRUSTING HEARTS.

"The Passion of the Christ" and Pain
"We did esteem Him...smitten of God and afflicted."—Isaiah 53:3 & 4

Mel Gibson's "Passion": showed our Savior's pain —
Oh yes, it was in truth quite well portrayed —-
But then it failed to cover in the main
What on the cross Christ suffered there one day.

Beyond the pain inflicted for our sin—
Intense indeed though that was seen to be—
Our Lord endured more than the pain of men;
He was forsaken of His God, we see.

Yes, suff'ring there was more than as a martyr—
Such as one Justin bore for Christ one day—
For God in wrath and righteous ardor
There smote The Son for sin—not HIS TO PAY!

"A Word to the Wise"
Jeremiah 36 with Revelation 22:18, 19

Jehoikim did rend the scroll
Of the prophet of God who averred
That all were damned, as all of old,
Who would choose to reject God's Word.

But the willful king then took with his hands
The shreds of that Word in his ire,
And, without any thought for God or for man,
With contempt tossed them into his fire!

The Book of Revelation states
To act as this king means it's true
That one takes from God's Word, and relates
Dire results of the Book thus his due!

Oh, my friends, with MY words you may play,
Cut and burn them and call them absurd;
But the king would now say if here talking today—
NEVER TRIFLE AT ALL WITH GOD'S WORD!

Love's Written in His Hands!
"I have engraved you on the palms of my hands…" – -Isa. 49:15, 16 NIV

Our Lord said we'd be hated sore
As He was in His day,
And so that hatred, known of yore,
IS manifest, I'd say!
Yes, Turkey's seen a case of late
Of inhumanity
So senseless that one must equate
It with brute savagery!

Disciples of the Muslim sect
There showed themselves to be
On brink of faith that would connect
With Christianity.

But just before prayer to our Lord
To come and make them whole,
The cultists rose to bind with cords
The three who'd save their souls!

The binding done, we understand
They set to "flay" with knives
Their victims, as per their Koran—
Scores of cuts descried!

In some details then later shown,
All fingers of six hands
Explicitly were slit as known
Prescribed in their Koran!

When help arrived to smash the doors,
The murderers took note
The time had come as tormentors
To slash their victim's throats!

In deaths quick time three spirits flew
To join in martyrs' bliss,
Awaiting where their bodies too
Would wake to Heaven's tryst!

But once more to this vale below
See Christ in God's command,
Whose heart, as all of His saints know,
Is measured by the hands.

Christ came on mission here to BLESS,
His life with LOVE so filled.
He helped and healed those in duress
To Satan's hurtful ills.

He went about in doing good—
But then in seeming loss,
He gave His life on beams of wood,
Suspended on a cross!

Dead then buried, yet He rose
To reign where hate is barred,
To pray for all—yes, even those
Who left His hands nail-scarred!

Christ died for sinners, Scriptures show—
That's what saints understand.
As for His church, we'll always know
LOVE'S WRITTEN IN HIS HANDS!

Jehovah-Jireh—Jesus-Provider
"And Abraham called the name of that place Jehovah-Jireh (The Lord will provide)"—Genesis 22:14

It's always been so one couldn't foreknow
The markets' wild dips up and down,
So involvement has woes—left me in the throes
Of bad debts, dogged doubts, shameful frowns!

Jehovah-Jireh, Jesus-Provider—
He's my Resource! I've life now brand new!
My future's much brighter! My heart is much lighter!
My Lord Jesus will now see me through!

Back then I can trace a weak faith, so misplaced,
Unfit for God's children, of course.
But now it's well-based, firmly fixed in God's grace—
Yes, my Jesus is now my Resource!

Jehovah-Jireh, Jesus-Provider—
He's my Resource! I've life now brand new!
My future's much brighter! My heart is much lighter!
My Lord Jesus will now see me through!

If you are oppressed and in this world distressed,
My dear Savior is there too for you!
In Christ there's success, if your sins you'll confess.
As He's blessed me, He'll surely bless you!

Jehovah-Jireh, Jesus-Provider -
He's my Resource! I've life now brand new!
My future's much brighter! My heart is much lighter!
My Lord Jesus will now see me through!

Is Jesus as "Son" Truly God?

Some say Jesus as "Son" can't be God,
For a son bespeaks weakness, they say.
In support I claim Christ was no fraud,
That as "Son" He our God is today!

Yes, in truth Jesus claimed deity,
When He told foes that He was "God's Son" (1)
But His foes pounced upon this, you see,
As a blasphemous sin of His tongue!

And indeed they were right technically,
For they knew "The True Son" men should laud, (2)
But were wrong when they judged Christ to be
Just a man—so He could not be God!

In His life Christ fulfilled ev'ry word
Of the prophecies made as to Him.
He at one time all honor observed
When He healed and forgave a man's sin. (3)

And in Hebrews there is a clear text
Which tells us that our Lord we should laud;
That His throne spans this world and the next,
For our God here cites Him as "O God"! (4)

(1) John 5:23; (2) Isaiah 9:6; (3) Mark 2:5-12; (4) Hebrews 1:8

Christ's Virgin Birth
John 8:41, 48 & 49

In Temple halls Christ found no friends,
Men's sympathies were lacking.
Christ only saw a bitter blend
Of faithlessness attacking.

The Pharisees and Sadducees
That day true hearts displayed.
Their malice could not be appeased
As Satan's protégés.

Their vitriol had reached its worst
In awful consummation
When they said, "We, as for OUR births,
Weren't born of fornication!"

Purport is seen in those dire words,
That He SO BORN had been,
This based on tales that gossips heard
And spread among men then.

More pointedly they named Him "Liar!"
And a "Samaritan!"
We'd gather they thought such His sire,
Had spawned the lie in Him!

Then Christ, "The Truth," gave His reply
With all due certainty:
"My Father sent me from on high,
And you dishonor Me!"

Now, friends, I ask, How shall foes stand
Who question here Christ's worth,
When He shall come with might at hand
To prove His virgin birth?

O Blest Heaven's Vision!
"We see Jesus"—Heb. 2:9; Job 19:26; 1 John 3:2b

O what delight, what saving sight
No other sight could match it!—
When first I saw the Lord My All,
Who brought me more than magic!

What "magic" can one's whole life span
To cancel sin's sad sorrow?
This Christ has come and is The One
"In sight" for each tomorrow!

The prophet Job at one time owed
So much to things men savored,
And yet he yearned—in fact all spurned—
To see "in flesh" His Savior!

The prophet John could see the Son—
And saints shall see in union—
When He shall come from martyrdom
To bring this world dominion!

Oh yes, I see and yet shall see
Him Who has saved my soul,
Who's brought me joy without alloy
And shall as eons roll!

And to you, friends, who see no end
To horrors here we rue,
Now look away to Christ today
For Heaven's vision too!

Jesus Is Our "Amen"

"These things saith the Amen, the Faithful and True Witness...."—Rev. 3:14a

Our Lord and Christ is named "Amen,"
And to that title's true,
Confirming all that's good for men;
And for Whom praise is due!

Yes, it's my pleasure to present
Christ, our eternal "Yes,"
The One from Whom we seek consent,
Whose faithfulness we bless!

Praise God, He is our Great High Priest
Who intercedes to cleanse!
His intercessions ever reach
Our God to save from sin!

As King all power He has won;
His edicts ever stand.
And no one ever dies unsung
Who clings to THIS King's hand!

As Prophet Jesus' words affirm
That which saints see in Him—
Especially His word confirms
"Ye must be born again!"
(John 3:5)

Christ is Our All in All, Even "Home"
John 14:6 & Psalm 90:1, 2

O friends, it's much we have in Christ—
Indeed, He's All in All—
But here I'd like to analyze
Some names by which He's called:

For wayward men Christ is "The Way"—
And so for seeking souls.
When by our Lord we're saved today,
His Heav'n becomes our goal!

Christ is "The Truth" to fill the mind—
With all good let it flood!
Such as forgiveness that we find
With cleansing through His blood!

He is our "Life" up from the dead—
That's death as Satan's slave!
Without Him ours is only dread,
And from both these we're saved!

And then as Moses says of Christ
"Forever God alone
Has been our Refuge from all sin
And 'Our Eternal Home'"!

Deliverance: Past, Present, and Future
2 Cor. 1:10

How great the Jesus whom I know
Who died to set men free!
His greatness lies in love He shows
Now and eternally.

This love, it's surely healed my past
And blesses present days;
It flows beyond to eons vast
To His eternal praise!

You wonder bow I can be sure
And have such peacefulness?
Well, friends, I know Christ's Word is sure,
And trusting it brings rest!

The Bible text, which I commend,
And which with joy I cite,
Is Second Corinthians one, verse ten.
Friends, here I'd share its light.

In this great text God's man named Paul
Tells of deliverance
From death which had him in its thrall,
Both awful and intense.

Moreover Paul saw Christ beyond—
Deliv'ring in the now,
And into days seen yet to dawn;
Whose love he surely vowed.

Well, friends, I'm done; the tale is told
Of this my confidence.
It's in the work that Christ unfolds:
Three-fold deliverance!

Got Jesus?
1 John 5:12

We have cares here today;
On our mind they do weigh;
And we've wants by the score that would please us.
But real needs we have few,
And, my friends, I'll tell you
IN YOUR GETTING MAKE SURE YOU'VE GOT JESUS!

Yes, He'll help with those cares,
As with Him you make prayers;
Read His word when old Satan would seize us.
So again I'll tell you,
With your sins so grave too,
IN YOUR GETTING MAKE SURE YOU'VE GOT JESUS!

O amen! And amen!
What a Savior He's been—-
Yes for all as He's come to relieve us!
Just say, "Jesus, right now
To Your Lordship I bow.
I ALSO WANT TO SAY, 'I'VE GOT JESUS!'"

Hey, now, didn't I say
He would help you today,
For He never has failed to receive us?
Now, just thank Him real good
As His child saved by blood,
AND THEN GO ON YOUR WAY—YOU'VE GOT JESUS!

Christ Is Jehovah God!

"Jehovah's Witness" they are called,
Yet Christ they do not laud,
Which leaves me puzzled, quite appalled,
Who knows His claim as God!
Yes, this I state as Bible based—
The Book of their appeal—
Christ's deity throughout is traced,
And herein now I'd deal.

Christ claimed to pre-date Abraham—
Which took His foes aback—
And claimed also to be "I AM,"
Provoking scribes attack.—1

They knew "I AM" as God's great name,
Redeemer of their nation,—2
So "blasphemy" was laid in blame
With death Christ's condemnation.—3

Some think as "Son" by definition
He lesser did remain,
But He disputed that condition—
Like power with God maintained!—4

In fact as "son of God" by name
Our Lord laid claim to be,
Which enemies saw as a claim
To God's equality.—5

He said, "I work as one with God—
Yes, so to raise the dead!"—6
For honor too He claimed men's laud
As truly God, their Head—7

In fact, dear friends, Him I applaud
And warn you as to Him:
That if you see Christ not as God
You'll perish forever in sin!—8

1 -John 8:58; 2 - Ex. 3:14; 3 -Matt. 26:65; 4 -John 5:23; 5 -John 5:18; 6 - John5:17; 7-John 5:23; 8 -"If you believe not that I AM you will die in your sins"—John 8:24.

Oh The Blood of Jesus!
1Peter 1:18, 19

I sing a song about Christ's Blood
With unique pow'r so true.
You see it's firmly Bible based,
And so my soul renews!

(1 John 1:9; Isaiah 1:18)
The Blood I sing it purges sin,
Though sins be crimson red.
They then are made as white as snow
Because my Savior bled!

(Exodus 12:7)
The Blood I sing preserves from death;
Hell's angels can't prevail!
This gift from God makes me secure;
Applied it ne'er can fail!

(Hebrews 10:29)
The Blood I sing it sanctifies,
Helps me to become pure.
It never yet has lost its pow'r,
And as such shall endure!

(Rev. 12:11)
The Blood I sing it overcomes
Together with a word
Of testimony to Christ's pow'r—
When enemies have heard!

(John 6:54)
The Blood at last shall take me Home
To Heaven's brotherhood.
And as I go I'll ever sing
About Christ's Precious Blood!

"Buddy"

From a story told by Edmund V. Cooke as found on the internet, about a dog that came to be a hero to American soldiers in Europe in World War I. The story is developed from a Christian perspective pointing up the love of our Lord Jesus Christ.

We didn't know just how he came
To join us in the war,
But he was welcomed just the same
As one almost at par.

Just a dog, he made a diff'rence though
In blessing each and all.
When beckoned ev'ryone would know
He'd come with just one call.

Yes, there he'd be to lick our hands,
His tail to wag in joy.
He'd even come 'cross no-man's-land
To bless some frightened boy.

"Buddy" we called him. No special breed.
But negatives, he had none.
Unwanted rations were his feed,
And most of us gave him some.

It's said this dog saved soldiers' lives,
Though medals he'd not won.
But this I know that I survived
Dire dangers since he'd come.

Now it's true in a war none will flourish—
And some perish all concur—
But dead or alive we all cherished
This angel in flesh and fur.

All said, our Buddy had real clout
As comrade till war's end;
And when survivors were mustered out,
This dog had come home with us then.

At port we all renewed our lives,
And nothing our joys could impede.
For Buddy, though—would he survive?
Seemingly no one gave him much heed.

And you can understand our changing
Since hell had giv'n way to peace.
Real life will see fresh arranging
When nightmares suddenly cease.

But two years down the road, I'd say,
From where I'd seen this dog last,
An M.D. "Hopeful" would one day
Have a visit from out of the past.

Yes, you see in doctors' lecture halls
We sometimes carved up beasts;
"vivisection" is what it's called—
A subject I like least!

This day, I now say in disgrace,
I looked at a table prepared
Where a common cur lay bound and in place—
Just cut open, and no one cared!

It's heart you could see was still pumping,
When it must have seen me in its pain;
Then it whined and its tail started thumping
As if joy were recalled once again!

Like Judas, the world's worst heretic
I reached out a hand toward that head—
And a tongue—Buddy's tongue—came out as to lick,
Then withdrew—and "Our Buddy" was dead.

Now, my friends, one hard lesson here I've learned—
Apart from my love of that dog:
At the cross we were loved by a love too—though spurned.
I've repented in glad epilogue.

"Herein is love, not that we loved God, but that He loved us and gave His Son to be the Peace Covering for all our sins."—1 John 4:10.

This Bridge Won't Let You Down
"Now unto Him be glory...now and forever, Amen."—Jude 1:24, 25.

When men on earthly bridges trust,
Is their trust justified?
Well, Minnesotans all say, "No!"
For fears were magnified

When one there spanning a broad stream
So suddenly came down,
With many injured critically,
And several, sadly, drowned.

This serves for us a lesson, friends,
As to uncertainty:
Events ahead now none can know,
Excepting casualties.

Of course, we hope our bridges here
will all tests surely pass;
And yet time proves they're not fail proof—
Except One unsurpassed:

God's Bridge O'er Woe-Filled Waters: He,—
A Man held in renown—
Christ Jesus never yet has failed—
This "Bridge" won't let you down!

The Most Beautiful Tree at Christmas
"His own self bore our sins in His body on the tree...."—1 Peter 2:24

The most beautiful tree at Christmas
Is the one upon which Jesus died.
Both its branches with scarlet resplendent
Hail Christ's Blood that sin's guilt surely hides.
And these branches, outstretched, are inviting
Each and all from attractions to rest
While all muse on God's love so exciting
And reflect on those resting here blest.
Indeed all in this tree sing with rapture
From their nests made secure in God's grace.
And you, too, sin-sick friend, cease from doubting
Choose the Christ of this tree to embrace!

CHAPTER TWO: POEMS ON GOD'S "SO GREAT SALVATION"

As yours truly has known the great influence of Jesus Christ upon the world of His creation, I begin this grouping of poems He has given me with my personal witness to "new birth" through His cross and resurrection. It all began wondrously for me on a Sunday, now more than seventy years ago, in an obscure little church in a small city in Oklahoma with the quaint American Indian name of "Muskogee." From that beginning at age twelve I have been blessed to go on as a minister of his for many years now (I am currently still ministering, at 83, in an adult Sunday school class in Jacksonville, Florida), gaining degrees from three schools of higher learning. From two of those schools Bible doctrine has been my emphasis, and throughout the following pages I relate some of those great tenets with which God has blessed me. May you too come to share in the blessings that have come to be mine.

I truly hope and pray in fact that if you have not had the experience of being "born again," as did I in that so long ago, that in the now you will enter into that blessed event as well. You surely may, and if but one person greets me in Heaven with the tidings of his/her personal salvation because of the influence in part through some poem or song of mine, how happy it will then make me! Indeed, friends, I believe the promise from God (Psa. 126:6) that "those who go forth weeping, bearing precious seed, shall doubtless come again with rejoicing, bringing their sheaves with them." I hang most hopefully on t hat little word "doubtless," believe with me!

With that hope before me, I commend the following poems on the death, resurrection, and ascension of Christ, precious parts of the "so great salvation" that so warm my heart as a student of Scripture.

On June the Ninth in 1940
John 3:5; Ephesians 2:1; 1 Peter 1:23, Revelation 20:15

The years have come, and they have gone—
Now moving in a spate—
Since that great day on June the ninth
When I knew Heav'n's birth date!

No, I'm not speaking of the day
On which my mother bore
Her fifth born (later numbr'ing nine!)—
This birth was so much more!

Oh, better had I not BEEN born
Of Mother and of Dad
Than go through life without THIS birth;
Outcomes would be so sad!

Our Lord has said that "from above"
We "must be born again"—
A Spirit-birth is what He meant,
Which surely saves from sin!

As sinners sin has slashed us all—
We're slain as by a knife!
Now all must hear our Savior's call
To pass from death to life.

To let this call fall on deaf ears
Means HERE we're barred from rest,
In these the quickly passing years—
And THEN eternal death!

But, friends, the awful dire events
Set forth here need not be;
Accept the Christ who died for you—
AND LIVE PERPETUALLY!

Providence, Predestination, and Free Will
Mathew 10:29-31; Proverbs 16:33; Genesis 22:13

How wonderful God's providence,
Provided from above!
And so we have much evidence
Of such sent down in love.

Friends, think of this, HAIRS ON OUR HEADS,
God knows their very number!
Which means He saw some lost in bed
Last night in our deep slumber!

O yes, it's true God knows our needs—
BUT ALSO THOSE OF BIRDS!
But as He for the birds takes heed,
More care for us occurs!

True, we and nations one and all
Are subject to our Lord:
Predestined, friends—AS DICE CUBES FALL,
We're made to worship Him!

That WE RESPOND, though, our God cares,
Invites us so to do.
When we're repentant, He hears prayer,
And blessing can ensue!

An early Bible case proclaims
How our God forgives sin:
When Abraham would remove shame,
A RAM GOD GAVE TO HIM!

This ram as TYPE OF CHRIST was viewed
To bear all sin away.
And Isaac too found life anew,
Much as we do today!

REAL HOPE and Timeless Happiness
Acts 16:16-20; Col. 1:27; Heb. 11:5

My friend, I ask, Do you have HOPE?
REAL HOPE, I mean today?
No, not that kind that's small in scope,
Which soon can pass away!
That sort of hope could be called "whim,"
Just "chance"—perhaps "caprice!"
With such a hope your future's dim;
It offers bogus peace!

In Philippi a maid on call
To offer psychic aid
Was source of hope for wealth's great haul
For one slave master's trade.
But she could sicken—even die!
And so give flight to cash!
In fact, she caught The Savior's eye—
So one's "great hopes" were dashed!

But, friends, REAL HOPE I'd here unfold,
Would put before you now:
This HOPE is sure, "as good as gold!"
As that which God endows!
This HOPE'S IN CHRIST, great Gift of God,
Who died for all our sins!
He lives, and if you'll give Him laud,
Eternal life you win!

Indeed, His HOPE remains "The Same"
Within to see us through.
And then when afterlife remains,
How great our rendezvous!
O yes, Christ's real! Our HOPE is real!
No more for me just "guess!"
O laud Him as YOUR HOPE—AND SEAL
ETERNAL HAPPINESS!

Good Works and Man's Salvation
Exodus 20:25; Ephesians 2:8, 9; John 6:29

The human heart is evil indeed
When boasting of its ways,
For Christ alone can meet man's need
In saving souls today.

From early records this is taught
In Israel's ancient schools:
With altar's need at Sinai sought
God clearly banned all tools!

There craftsmen wanted to display
Their skills to build for men,
But God said, "Put your tools away!
They have no part herein!

"If on my altar tools are used
Where cleansing sin's the aim,
I here declare it's been abused—
My altar's been profaned!"

Such is in keeping with the words
Of the Apostle Paul;
He taught that works are most absurd
To save—God bars them all!

And Jesus said, "The work of God
For which He's bade consent
Is that we give His Son the Laud,
Have faith in Him Who's sent."

If You Should Die Tonight
Luke 23:39-43

Friend, if you should die tonight,
Your soul should take its flight,
Where then would your soul be
For all eternity,
Saved or lost? Oh what cost
Hangs on uncertainty!

But here a case I'd give
That teaches we can live
In peace forevermore
With Christ the Lord Adored,
Have joy without alloy
And Heav'n's real hope in store!

A thief once on a cross
Knew not the dreaded loss
That waited with his death
With only minutes left!
What did he do to teach me and you
God's way to Heaven blest?

He noted to his side
One also crucified
In peace, a sign o'er His Head:
"Jesus, King of the Jews," it read.
Confessing his sin, he then cried to Him,
"Remember me, Lord, up ahead!"

What joy that I now tell;
Christ loved this man so well!
Though He Himself in pain,
He pledged this other's gain—
Beyond all price gave him paradise,
That's Heaven, God ordained!

Oh, judgment's ever near!
Yes, God's word makes it clear
If Heaven there we crave,
The guilt must here be waived!
Avoid the knell that calls to Hell—
Our Savior still will save!

But I would interpose,
A caution add for those
Who plan as though "God gives
Yet many years to live!"—
Oh, death can come e'er this day is done,
AND IN DEATH OUR GOD CANNOT FORGIVE!

JUST ONE, Lest Presuming Men Rue
Luke 23:32-43

Oh the saddest of most tragic words
Which two men on this earth could have heard
Are those saying, "Alas,
'The harvest is past'
With dead men when the body's interred!"

But true hope on two crosses remained,
Which each sinner way back there could claim,
That to wit on one cross
Our Lord hung for their loss,
So each, living, could Heaven still gain.

O praise God, it forever is true
That one man at death's door through God knew
Christ's promise divine
Of Heaven sublime—
But JUST ONE, lest presuming men rue!

Yes, it's true our sin nature's so bad,
Blest results facing death oft aren't had;
For with sin the heart's seared,
and the mind's filled with fear—
So that RARELY Christ then makes men glad!

Five Brides of Genesis and Christ's Church

Of great int'rest to me it's recorded
About brides of five men I've researched,
That in Genesis these are accorded
Many typical ties to Christ's church:

First of all, Adam's bride, our first mother,
Was brought forth here to live from His side.
So our Lord, on the cross as no other
Gave His flesh AND WE LIVE as His bride!

And Rebecca for Isaac showed FAITH
PLUS GOOD WORKS which took her many miles
To wed Isaac unseen—and that, yes, apace!
So the church shows such faith all the while!

And in Leah see Jacob's sad mate;
Often TESTED she was through her life,
But she seemed to bear up against fate,
And in birthing of souls surely thrived!

Then the last of great women I'd name
Asenath, Joseph's wife, at his side—
LIKE THE CHURCH GENTILE BORN WITH NO FAME!—
SHE IS ONE WITH HER LORD AS HIS BRIDE!

The Triune God in My Salvation

The Father's wisdom furnished it, my soul's salvation plan;
The Spirit further fosters it, my sinful will to ban;
But Christ's blood finalizes it, for ev'ry faith-filled man;
With Peter wisely teaching it, as God's historian!

"To the elect...according to the foreknowledge of God the Father,
through the sanctifying work of the Holy Spirit for obedience to Jesus
Christ and the sprinkling of His blood."
—1 Peter 1:1, 2

Faith and Works Are Wed
1 John 2:19; James 2:19; Romans 10:10.

A controversy has gone on
For many, many years;
Results have been with saints upset
And sometimes, too, in tears.

One side says saints are saved by faith,
That's faith in Christ alone.
The other says were saved by works;
This point of view well known.

But actually true faith and works
I see go hand in hand.
The Scriptures show they're "wed" as such,
United in God's plan!

Ephesians two verse eight with ten
Will here present God's voice:
The faith that saves with works behaves
According to His choice.

So when "the saved" backslides to say,
"This sainthood's not for me!"
His faith it wasn't wed with works,
So barren, yes, he'd be!

In fact I'd say that this man's faith,
From brain cells made no start,
For Scripture says of faith that saves
It goes right to one's heart!

There's No Assessing of "Double Jeopardy!"

God's wrath is held in tension
Like storms held back at sea—
But oh the apprehension
Should such come shore on me!

Forecasters all predict it,
And sinful I'm in line;
It's foolish to conclude that
Wrath won't touch me sometime!

But, yes, I've trusted Jesus
Who died once for my sins.
You say, "His suff'ring frees us
From judgment's discipline"?

You're right, Christ took our place
To bear God's wrath alone,
But with His gifts of grace
EARTH'S PROBLEMS still are known!

But for my gift in blessing
'Gainst Hell RIGHT NOW, I see—
God's wrath knows no assessing
Of "double jeopardy!"

Gleaning for Life's Meaning
Gen. 35; Psa. 51; John 9; Acts 26; Matt. 11:28

When times distress with men perplexed
Let us for wisdom glean
Where faith brings hope, enlarging scope
Of Heaven so pristine.

Let's take long looks through God's Good Book
With those who've found the way;
For there it's shown what they have known
That faith will win the day.

Yes, Bible gleaning has had true meaning
For men for untold years;
So for our sakes, lives to remake,
Let's glean negating tears.

Good Joseph, Jacob's son, o'er evil forces won,
Though facing such at ev'ry turn.
He saw the worst, through God reversed
As favor was confirmed.

King David failed, by sin impaled,
Then wept in earnest prayer.
Oh hear him laud his gracious God
For cleansing he found there!

The man born blind with steady mind
Found wrangling so intense;
But still, said he, "Through Christ 1 see!"—
This borne from common sense!

There's Paul, a Jew, who Christians slew,
Yet through true faith endured.
Thrown to the ground, there His Lord found,
And ministry assured.

And last a verse, so true yet terse,
For all sin leavened to view:
Christ down life's road will carry your load;
He died for me and you!

A Dinnertime Tale

It was sad just how Tom and his Jan had last parted,
And recalling it now makes a teardrop to start.
She had faulted this man whom with love she regarded.
Now a dinner she made to prove truly her heart.

There was succulent beef, creamy whipped mashed potatoes,
Corn-on-the-cob, and hot rolls in a row,
Milk gravy so good, and of course sliced tomatoes,
Creamed peas and lime pie, 'cause Tom liked it, you know.

Well, he said he would come at the hour of six,
But the hour arriving on this fateful night,
He called on the phone, said, "My mind's in a fix;
I will try to come later,"—but sense took its flight!

He up joined the Marines, if the truth one would know.
And the days turned to months and the months into years.
But Tom never forgot her, said he still loved her so.
And Jan still loved him too; this in spite of her tears.

Twenty years came and went—bringing them close to forty.
His head was most bald, and gray hairs—she had some.
They neither had married, for each felt so sorry
For those faults long ago when they both were so young.

Well, one day as a salesman Jan's town Tom was in,
And hearing a song about "...lovers' hearts riven,"
He thought that if he would be named among men,
Then he must on her call and ask to be forgiven.

His emotions were suffering an unusual mix
When the time set brought him to her door as of old.
Then she answered the bell, said, "I see it is six.
Do come in, my dear Tom, lest our dinner grow cold."

There was succulent beef, creamy whipped mashed potatoes,
Corn-on-the-cob, and hot rolls in a row,
Milk gravy so good, and of course sliced tomatoes,
Creamed peas, and lime pie, 'cause Tom liked it, you know.

O dear God, help us all through our lives to be keeping
Short accounts both with You and then too with each loved one—
Lest the days turn to months, and long years find us grieving
With those haunting regrets when life's race is near run!

"None of Ours Is Lost!"
Genesis 14; Luke 15:4; John 17:12

There they're hying, foes defying,
Moving through the sea
Past all sinning, they're for winning
Total victory!

God gets glory in the story
Of that Hebrew host.
Moses leading, they're succeeding,
Mounting Sinai's coast!

Now they're hailing their prevailing
All the way across!
Hear them yelling, praises swelling—
"None of ours is lost!"

Prophesying Another's vying
Against their ancient foe.
Jesus leads forth that from henceforth
Vic'try we may know!

O the Trickster met our Victor
On a cruel tree!
And forever we've a Savior—
Hey, we're also free!

Here's enhancement of advancement
O'er Satan and sin's loss
We enthuse with early Jews
"NOT ONE OF OURS IS LOST?"

God's Elect and Me
2 Thess. 2:13; 1 Peter 1:1, & 2

The Lord, my friend, has chosen folk
In this community
Who must be snatched out of the yoke
Of their captivity,

So they'll escape the fire and smoke
Which all the lost shall see!

We do not know whom God elects
Of man's fraternity,
Nor do these folk themselves suspect
Glad is their lot to be;
But this we know, EACH MUST CONNECT
WITH CHRIST IN TIME IF FREED!

Yet it's for us who know the Lord
To seek these earnestly,
Though they may curse, call us abhorred—
Yes, threaten you and me!
But O the joy in Christ the Lord
With their faith's victory!

So up, my soul and blest of God,
To call—and constantly!—
Those who are His here and abroad
To leave their misery.
We must in this give Christ the Laud—
WE ONCE WERE LOST LIKE THESE!

"Lord, This Is What You Said"

Dear Lord of All Our Righteousness,
Please help that we will be
In likeness with that honesty
That's Yours eternally.

And, also, Lord, as we would want
That men OUR word believe,
Please help that we'll ne'er question here
YOUR Word which we've received.

Then we shall be like one of old
Who on Your Word did dwell,
Reminding that one time You'd said
That You would treat him well.

And then again, at later date,
He feared Esau's ill will,
But with God's Word and faith well placed
He saw sweet peace prevail.

With that last thought I'd emphasize
The point to bring it home,
Here stressing that we should be wise
With Jacob's way our own—

To give God's Word priority,
Recalling it with care;
That in our tests we'll let it be
A real part of our prayer.

"O Lord,...You promised to treat me kindly and multiply my descendants. Please Rescue me from my brother Esau!"
—Gen. 32:12, 13

Two Webs Woven

"An awful web we start to weave
When first we cheat or first deceive;
By such we know entrapments here
That brings distress beyond all cheer!"

Oh, yes, 'tis true, but now I'd tell
Of one small web that served man well.
This one involved an incident
Where God's Good Hand was evident.
In World War Two an air force ace
Was shot down from the skies and faced
A searching party with a will
To capture him intent to kill.
Well, he too seeking self to save
Found respite in a little cave.
In that small space he heard without
The foe encircling all about.
"Oh, God," he prayed, "please make a wall
To hide me here, frustrating all!"

Then in dim darkness he perceived
A little spider start to weave.
In just a while the airman saw
Its work well done, it did withdraw.
So quickly then he was aware
Of one who came to seek him there,
Who saw a web before his cave,
Who must have thought, "My time I'll save;
He's not in there, for I can see
A spider here a web did weave."
The foe retreated and the airman raised
So quietly paeans of praise:
"O God, you heard my feeble call:
That spindly web became my wall!
O thanks to You, Your providence;
That spider was your angel sent!"

"And so, dear friends, my tale is told.
In two webs here two truths unfold:
Though hurtful webs men often weave,
Our God weaves too, I do believe!"

"Up" or "Down"?

Should I go "up" or in death "down"?
Depends on what's endorsed.
My test below may raise a frown
But save from sad remorse:

"What have I done with Jesus Christ?"
This question asks it all.
Christ stands twixt darkness and the light,
And, friend, such is "our call!"

The sin cursed for all time will fit
With Korah as their kind,
For Korah went to death's dark pit
In pride of sinful mind!

Opposed to his case I would cite
One for a better test,
The publican pled that he might
From sin be saved and blest.

Now, sinner-friend, we're sinners all—
In either one such case.
If proud we wait our final fall;
If humble we find grace.

A little prayer will change our frown
(If changed we want to be):
"Oh, save me, Christ; I'd not go 'down';
Instead 'up' is my plea!"

If, friend, you prayed that simple prayer,
Since Christ died in our place
But then arose, our God declares
We're saved from sin's disgrace!

"What then will you do with Jesus, who is called The Christ?" Matt. 27:22; "...Now it came to pass...that the ground split apart under them, and the earth opened its mouth and swallowed them up...all the men with Korah..."—Num. 16:32, 33; "And the tax collector, standing afar off, would not so much as raise his eyes to heaven, but beat his chest, saying "God be merciful to me a sinner!"...This man went to his house justified (redeemed—JE)."—Luke 18:13,14

My Faith this July Fourth

It's said, "We're not a Christian nation"—
Some "notables" affirm—
Yet this calls for negation—
We're still such, my concern!

It's borne out in our history:
We early made Christ Lord;
And then we won, no mystery,
A place in world accords!

When nations issued S.O.S.,
We helped arch foes subdue;
Sent foods to others in distress;
Brought medical help too.

We've blessed the nation Israel,
Since God in Scriptures urged;*
Have helped her in the physical
While others sang her dirge!

We've lived out hist'ry gen'rously—
Sent untold wealth abroad -
And now we're "Christian" not to be?
Can't name our Christ as God?

O yes, it's true we've wandered too,
Have shamed Christ to His Face—
But we've not ALL forsaken Him;
A remnant pleads His grace!

Our God's the selfsame God of yore
Who Sodom would have saved;
If but a remnant Him adored,
His wrath would not have raged!**

And surely we've a remnant here
In this wide land across,
All sharing in His mercy's cheer,
Forgiven through His cross!

So in this day when some folks hedge,
The faithful hail Your worth.
And I pledge Lord – yes, GLADLY pledge –
My faith this July Fourth!

*Genesis 12:1
**Genesis 18:26

"The Impossible" Is Still Possible!

The lowly crow could never know
The rare heights nor the flight of the eagle.
Nor could the wren in looks contend
With the beautiful peacock so regal.

Much less can man before God stand
In his flesh and claim entrance above—
Unless—amen!—he's been "born again"*
And cleansed from his sin through Christ's love.

Now, friend, I ask you your life to review:
See if one day back there you could name
When on that day for sure you can say,
"I was cleansed from my sin and its stain!"?

If not I avow you can even now
Take Christ Jesus as Savior from sin.
He died surely for you so that good could ensue—
So indeed you could be "born again!"

"Marvel not that I said unto you, 'You must be born again!'"—Jesus Christ, John 3: 3

God's Great Invitation to "Come!"
Genesis 7:1; Isaiah 1:18; Matthew 11:28; Revelation 22:17, 20

The most crucial of all invitations is "Come!"
Come to God for life's greatest of tests.
See if He in His love does not for you become
The Good Giver of life at its best.

For an instance see Noah with family of eight
Come aboard when God called from The Ark.
Then while shutting the door it's believed He did state,
"You are mine, Heaven bound; death you'll thwart!"

Next when called "Come to reason" God said men should know
That their sins grown so grievous are gone.
Though like scarlet and crimson they'd be "white as snow"
Through forgiveness in Christ—now well known!

Then invited to come to this same Christ as Lord,
There we find that all striving does cease.
Our God gives harmony in His mix of accords;
Yes, sweet rest in His message of peace!

One more case: the last book, Revelation, does state
God's last call—and yet all here intone—
"Come for God's greatest nectar your thirst e'er to slake."
And "Come, Lord, make Your Heaven our Home!"

"All Things Are Yours!"
1 John 3:21-23

Some say, You've lost the best of life!"
I say you've gained it all in Christ!
"All things are yours!" the Spirit said,
Since Christ your Lord rose from the dead!
Yes, death is yours—for you Christ died!
Sin's gone thereby, you're justified!
You've conquering pow'r for time secured,
God's love and Heaven thus assured!
To clinch it all your God is just,
And so you have His Word in trust
That surely grace on you He pours!
Reemphasized, "All things are yours!"

The "Exceeding Abundantly Able" God

One verse has blessed my soul aplenty;
It's found in Ephesians there.
It's chapter three and then verse twenty;
And its lessons I'd now with you share.

Our God has great ability—
"Exceeding abundant" in fact.
He answers pray'r most readily,
And briefly His wonders I'd track.

When Israel fled a bondage haunting,
With Moses in leadership sound,
They crossed a sea, its depths most daunting—
And praise God, it was crossed "on dry ground!"—(1)

When these same folk in fact were facing
A dreadful foe midst fears so dire,
The army's pow'r God nixed, erasing
All that foe—indeed with a choir!—(2)

General Gideon had his large army,
But large numbers with God wouldn't do;
So he sent some back home by the thousands—
And decisively won with a few!—(3)

Christ's crowds with hunger activated,
In the wild found no food there in store;
But Christ met their huge needs—all were sated,
And big baskets remained for the poor!—(4)

When on a cross the guilty sinner
Asked the Lord that some day he'd be blessed,
Jesus said, "O, TODAY you're a winner;
On this day you shall know Eden's best!"—(5)

Sinner friend, haste to know One you'll savor;
All who've known Christ in this life have won.
Cease from sin; take Him now as your Savior,
And FOREVER YOU'LL WIN WITH THE SON!—(6)

(1) Exod. 14; (2) 2 Chron. 20; (3) Judges 7; (4) Matt. 14; (5) Luke 23;
(6) John 3

"Tsunamis" Break Deep from the Breast
Proverbs 4:23

King David's day had been routine.
Of late they'd all gone well.
If only he'd been made aware
Of demon plans in hell!

Inaction, that's the devil's boon,
A gift giv'n him outright!
So David with his armor shelved
Was unprepared for fight.

His day, it started peacefully,
No hint of that in store.
"Tsunamis" break deep from the breast—
Yes, from the ocean floor!

O David never should have gazed
With lust there in his heart.
When waves broke forth they broke so much—
Hell has such little starts!

There's Ammon, Tamar, and Absolom,
All fell, to name but three,
Yet many, many more would fall
Before that awful sea!

And looking back we can rehearse
A saying among men,
That is, "But for one lust-filled look
It might have never been!"

"Keep your heart with all diligence, for out of it spring the issues of life."—Prov. 4:23

God's Zeal
"Zeal for your house has consumed me."—John 2:17, Psalm 69:9

The greatest trait of God is love
With limitless appeal.
But one off-shoot,
An attribute,
That complements is zeal.

And so God's love for Israel
Is known historically.
Also His zeal
Is there most real.
It's shown so wondrously.

A case in point: We've lately read
How doubters failed in test.
They couldn't heed
How God could feed
His hungry hordes with flesh.

But He in His omnipotence
Brought quail to reap in heaps.
With lusts applied
None from them shied—
But see some later weep?

Oh, let's today hold it as true
About the love of God,
That it's endorsed—
Indeed finds force
In holy zeal we laud.

There's Power with God in an "If"
2 Kings 7:3-20

Four poor lepers were starving like many that day
As the Jews suffered siege in the city.
They knew time was so short, that so soon they'd be dead,
And their deaths would evoke little pity.
So they thought on the legions outside 'round the walls
Fully armed there to thwart their escape,
That this foe fully fed MIGHT THROUGH GOD YET HAVE GRACE;
Yes, oh yes, it's a chance they must take!

They'd go forth to this foe, those who surely could kill,
And perchance a few crumbs they might give!
"We have odds next to nil over there—SURELY HERE!
IF GOD WILLS, WITH SOME CRUMBS WE SHALL LIVE!"

So with hearts beating wildly—but bated in breath—
The four struggled to mount the great wall.
Then they limped to a scene that was eerily still!
Nothing moved! Not a breath! Like a pall!

It was clear that the foe had deserted the camp!—
But the best in good food yet was there!
Yes, choice food! Precious food everywhere for their eating!
Much in drink also found—oh, what fare!

One can't know the great joy the four shared in those moments—
Until shame, conscience borne on them came.
They with haste must return once again to the city,
The great news to the starving proclaim!

So informed, all the Jews with great ecstasy known—
Though most weak—to that camp quickly ran!
God in grace had displaced their most terrible foe,
GIVEN FOOD—EVEN GOLD IN COMMAND!

Yes, their foe fearing help for the Jews was oncoming,
Left their hoard with their swords, for the hills!
So today sinners can with their need on God calling
STILL WITH FAITH, LITTLE FAITH, BE FULFILLED!

And it's clear God's most near those most needing His mercy—
For salvation it's 'specially true—
But again, WITH FAITH'S 'IF,' SO LIKE SEED OF THE MUSTARD,*
GOD OBSERVES, HEARS THAT WORD, LIFE'S RENEWED!

*Matthew 17:20; 6:37

Mephibosheth Was Like Ourselves
2 Sam 4:4; 9:1-11

Mephibosheth, much like ourselves
In body was so weak.
With little strength to help himself,
He others' aid did seek.

When but a child Mephibosheth
Midst war was caused to fall.
When yet unborn we knew true death
Through Adam's guilt, recall.

And so of him and us it's said
We're harmed by other's wrong;
So likewise we must look for aid
To others who are strong.

Mephibosheth found for his friend
King David on his throne;
And our Best Friend, a True Godsend,
Is Christ Whose Blood atones.

The crippled man when bade to come
Responded as a guest;
So there in grace he found his place
As fam'ly fully blest!

Yes, we too hear a call most clear
To sit at Jesus' table.
With needs most dear 'mid family there
In grace we're found most able!

An Empty Eggshell

At Christian School Jay Tillman was the victim
    Of sickness which predicted death ahead.
    In second grade, he was a "special student"
With normal children, which had caused some dread.

You see, he was much older than his classmates.
    With twisted body, problems were not small;
He drooled and bothered those that were about him
    By noises made, his presence hind'ring all.

Ms. Smith, his teacher, was so dedicated
    To children's learning—yes, and to Jay's too.
So Christmastime she telephoned the Tillmans,
    Arranged to look at progress in review.

She counseled saying, "Folks, Jay needs attention,
    Which in our class I find so hard to give.
A special group at school would be more helpful.
    He'd prosper there so well, I'm positive."

"Oh, Ma'am, please don't!" they quickly interjected,
    "For such a move would be Jay's devastation!
He loves you so, and all those in your room—
Please, let's just pray with greater concentration!"

Ms. Smith, conceding parents should know better
    As to a move and what it might entail—
    Especially concerning "devastation"—
    Decided that their wishes should prevail.

And so the class went on without a change—
    Except more prayer suggested seemed to help.
    Yes, Jay had evidently progressed better.
More peacefulness seemed there within himself.

Some months then passed and Easter lay ahead
    With emphasis upon Christ's Resurrection.
    Ms. Smith, preparing for a Bible lesson,
Desired her students have a real connection,

So for a contest she brought sev'ral eggshells
(Just plastic ones) and stated for a task
That students find some Resurrection symbols,
Then in their eggshells bring them back to class.

One day saw twenty eggshells all turned in;
One from each student showed their eagerness:
A snake skin, acorn, spent balloon, and flower,
A rock with moss—all these and more, impressed.

The teacher for the entries made some comments,
She saying these indeed had blessed her so,
As they had touched somehow on Resurrection
(But Jay's was empty. Why she didn't know).

She then prepared to move on with that said,
When Jay, sad faced, spoke up somewhat disturbed:
"Ms. Smith, is my eggshell not any good?
You didn't say it was with your last words."

"But, Jay," rejoined the teacher with concern,
"You didn't have a thing there in your shell!
I couldn't make remarks since it was empty."
Said Jay, "Then nothin's good then, I can tell.

"Jesus said they'd look but wouldn't find Him,*
When they looked for Him when they saw He's dead.
Isn't nothin' somethin' in this story?
I thought it was a lot up in my head."

Ms Smith, agape, looked at her brilliant student.
"Why Jay, you're right!" she said as one quite stunned.
"Yes, NOTHINGS REALLY SOMETHING in Christ's story—
And for your shell I'd say first prize you've won!"**

Well, this our tale of Jay is almost ended,
Except to say in May Jay fell and passed away.
And at his gravesite nineteen students placed there
ONE LARGE BUT EMPTY EGGSHELL, seen today.

A final word in postscript to this story
As to the body where our Jay shall dwell.
It shall be LIKE HIS LORD'S IN WONDROUS SPLENDOR*** -
LIKEWISE HIS GRAVE AS EMPTY AS THAT SHELL!****

*John 7:34 with 8:21; **Matt. 21:16;(j)***John 3:2; ****1 Thess. 4:16

God, Too, Worked at that Scene!
Matthew 1:5

Ruth, widowed as a maid,
Was sent out to the fields,
While kin, Naomi, stayed
To pray with strong appeal
That needs might be allayed
In harvest's gen'rous yields.

Some say that it was luck
That sent her out to glean
Where Boaz' men undertook
To pick the fields quite clean.
But, no, it wasn't luck—
God, too, worked at that scene!

And so Boaz, attending,
Saw Ruth's sure gleaning there
And asked of her, intending
To show to her his care.
He learned of His kin's sending
Her out for their welfare.

He then began inquiring
To remedy their case,
As kinsman, law requiring
He should their cares erase—
And oh, its so inspiring—
He wed Ruth in God's grace!

But I'd reveal this news,
Their best was yet to be,
For Moabitess Ruth
Became in history—
NAMED IN CHRIST'S LINE OF TRUTH,
HIS GENEALOGY!

Matthew 1:5

Just Where on "Resurrection" Are You?

Just where on "resurrection"
Are you, I ask, my friend?
Be wise to make inspection
As to your future end.

An aid to apt detection
As to your place I'd give
With view to aid correction
If you for Christ would live.

If you've no predilection
For Christ Who died for you,
You stand in sad defection
With NO GOOD END in view.

But those with Christ's connection
In this life with His Word
Will have God's sure protection
And Heaven thus assured.

But sadly for reflection,
If you reject Christ's cross,
By God your own rejection
Precedes your total loss.

If you here urge exception
To what I cite above,
I plead real circumspection
To note God's Word, Who loved.

Yes, loved you in election
Of His cross to insure
That you by your selection
Through Him could Hell abjure!

Of Us and Them
Matthew 5:44

Concerning us and terrorists,
Who scorn a love for man,
We must check all by Bible texts,
Just how with God men stand.

They say to get to Paradise,
"Let's kill the infidels!"
While our God's Son paid our sin's price;
His death fully prevails!

And God's Word teaches He is Love;
Theirs surely teaches hate.
So in the name of God above,
Can we to them relate?

Well, I'm sure, friends, of us and them
As God loves all, we're told;
That we should love as we're loved, friends;
Love surely will save souls!

Yes, we should give the Gospel out
In love for these our foes.
It's prayer that will turn them about
As "born again," transposed!

Hey, I'm a "WHOSOEVER!"
Revelation 22:17

I am not your most wise or your wittiest guy
(Yes, I've often found "egg on my face").
It's for sure I'm a sinner and so wonder why
That my God should save me by grace.

Well, the Bible before me, I only find sense
For an answer in His Word, you see:
Christ my God with a love beyond measure, intense,
Freely died on His cross JUST FOR ME!

O, I know the whole world was the aim of His love—
And no doubt billions share in its thrill—
But good news from the Gospel says Christ from above
Came to save "WHOSOEVER here will!"

Well, hey, I'm "WHOSOEVER," was there in great need
In my home town by nature undone;
And so glad as a lad of but twelve to take heed
To God's call, "WHOSOEVER" may come!

"And the Spirit and the bride say, Come, And let him that heareth say, Come. And let him that is athirst come. And whosoever will let him take the water of life freely."
— Revelation 22:17.

Hey, Who's Holding Whom?

Can "sheep" turn into "goats?"
Well, that has evoked much
In way of saints' suggestions,
And here I'd address such:

One commentator said,
"A saved man, indeed, might
At daybreak be 'in Christ,'
But 'out and lost' that night!"

He said, "To Christ as Savior
You must cling till the end!"
To sheep of this poor shepherd I'd say,
Hold tight to Christ, my friends!

But I prefer that other
Who said we'd persevere
"Because Christ does the holding;
To those whom He deems dear!"

You've heard about the youngster
Who ice-bound clung to Dad;
He slipped while he was holding,
And so fell hard, quite sad!

So Dad said, "Hey there, youngster,
Just see what we have done?
I feel we'll both fare better—
If I'd hold your hand, son!"

Yes, friends, a stronger Hand
Holds us, so we're secure.
In fact, BOTH GOD AND SON
MAKE HIS SAINTS DOUBLY SURE!

Please, do read John 10:27-30!

Our Saddest War Had Ended
1 Corinthians 15:3b; Romans 1: 15, 16

Our Civil War had ended;
All slaves were now set free,
So freedom's song ascended,
In praise of victory!

Lincoln, the liberator,
For this great cause had died,
Martyred by souls embittered
For lusts left unsupplied.

But also it's recorded,
"Abe's Gift" from slav'ry's chains
For some was not reported—
So these in "chains" remained!

Their pains as yet unmet!
What utter travesty!
With others' joys unchecked,
These still in slavery?!?!

Yet in a larger measure—
Yes, on a worldwide scale—
How sad that saints let fester
Souls lost and bound for hell!

Not telling of the Savior,
"Our Lincoln" Who has died?
Are we not worse for favor
Who've put love's pow'r aside?

Oh yes, His life's been given—
"Emancipator's" Blood—
And so all bonds are riven!
Men freed through Christ, Our God!

Yes, we set free are debtors
Like Paul in years gone by,
To air God's better "letter"
That states Our Savior died!

Of course some will do nothing,
Will choose the well-worn way,
But for those slaves neglected
We challenge saints today.

O take the proclamation
"In chains ALL are set free!
Christ Jesus loves all nations;
TO ALL GRANTS SIN'S REPRIEVE!"

A Kiss Can Be a Door

The Israelites oft times received
God's truths in metaphor,
And so we see a kiss as such
At times can be a door—

A door by which we can invite
The Lord into our lives;
Also by which, through love's embrace,
We cause our love to thrive.

Well, since before I've used that door
To take as Lord my Christ,
I now, as did the Shulamite,
Kiss to keep love alive.

"Kiss the Son, lest you perish from the way, when His wrath is kindled but a little."—Psalm 2:12; "Let Him kiss me with the kisses of His mouth, for Thy love is better than wine."—Canticles 1:2.

On Rushing to Judgment

In matters of serious import,
Say the wisest of all our wise men,
Never should one rush to judgment
Till all of the data are in.

In one case that I'm made aware of,
In time many long years ago,
An incident took place in England
Which to this point seems most apropos.

Across from the channel in Europe
Two gen'rals were locked in great war:
Wellington, of his fair England,
And Napoleon, warfare's French czar.

Now the English awaited the outcome
With int'rest absorbing them all,
But ign'rance for lack of late tidings
Held each Brit under its numbing pall.

At length came a slow sailing vessel
From the mainland with long-waited news,
Which, wig-wagged ahead by flag signals,
First left people greatly confused:

"WELLINGTON DEFEATED...," it spelled out,
Then a mantle of fog came between,
With conclusion, "Our army's defeated!—
What dishonor for our side this means!"

But then later the fog's mantle lifted;
The ship's message came spelled out once more:
"WELLINGTON DEFEATED THE ENEMY!"—
And great joy burst upon England's shores!

For us now there's a message of Calv'ry
And of Death which was there dealt our Lord:
First, "JESUS DEFEATED...," was spelled out,
And our hearts seemed as pierced by a sword!

But then soon came that great Lord's Day Morning
When the Father's full message came clear:
"JESUS DEFEATED THE ENEMY!"—
WHAT A DIFF'RENCE! WHAT JOY! OH WHAT CHEER!

"Christ died for our sins...was buried...and He arose again the third day...."
—1 Corinthians 15:3.4

In Wrath, Lord, Remember Your Mercy
Habakkuk 3:2

"Lord, revive now your work in the midst of the years,"
    In this age surely lost as no other!
Untold millions have died—with few shedding their tears—
    Doomed to death in the wombs of their mothers!

An obsession with sex, too, has gripped my fair land,
    Even leaders corrupting young minds!
Sex slaves seized, homes are grieved all at lust's dire demands—
    With our youth caught for sure in the grind!

See the murders, the mayhem, such evil contrived—
    The likes of which never was seen:
Hatchet slayings, beheadings, some buried alive!—
    Oh, do tell me, "It's only a dream!"

See the gambling, the drugs and the booze in consumption,
    The pleasure-prone throngs gone insane!
Oh, where now, I say, is the once-held assumption
    That our land is "God's Christian domain"?

Oh the motto of many is, "I will get mine!"
    Mesmerized by The Lotto the masses;
And beyond see law suits and gross schemes hatched "on line,"
    With the shameless evading just taxes!

Notwithstanding all said, I'm still loving this nation;
    So for judgment, I plead, Lord, don't hurry!
But revive us, I pray, granting gracious salvation;
    Oh, "in wrath, Lord, remember your mercy!"

Am I "A Pancake Half-Baked"?
"Ephraim is a cake unturned...!"—Hosea 7:8

Our God says in His Word
We should not be absurd,
Saying sanctification
Is just our avocation!
So lived Ephraim of old,
Whom God roundly did scold
As a fry-cook's mistake,
As "a pancake half-baked!"

The in-crowd in Christ's day
Lived as those gone astray.
Pious deeds some were done,
Yet true love few had some!
Like a cake one side burned,
Their need was to be turned.
This conclusion I'd make:
They were cakes, too—"half-baked!"

Am I "a pancake half-baked,"
Making Ephraim's mistake?
On one side am I burned
While the other's unturned?
Hypocrites don't fare well—
Sometimes ending in hell!
Our God savors no cake
That's like Ephraim—"half-baked!"

Don't be a fry-cook's mistake!
Don't be "a pancake half-baked,"
On one side perhaps burned
While the other's unturned!
Walk a walk circumspect, one your God can respect.
This inspection let's make:
AM I "A PANCAKE HALF-BAKED?"

1 Know that I by Grace Shall Make It!
Luke 22:31; Hebrews 7:25; John 10:30; Romans 8:26

I know that I by grace shall make it,
Though trials test me "down the line."
My future's sure; on this I'll stake it:
My Lord prays for me all the time!

O yes, He's One with God the Father,
Who works in concert with The Son.
A Power Pact quite like these others
Who clinch the nails when vict'rys won!

And here I'm grateful as a Christian
For triple grace that God has shown—
The Spirit too has been commissioned
To pray for me, His pow'r well known!

Such wondrous truth makes me more prayerful.
This Triune God deserves my best.
In gratitude I'll be most careful
Till Heav'n I enter, past all tests.

Caregivers and "Our Good Samaritan"

Thank God for dear caregivers through the years
Who've been our help, at times our life and stay;
Who've lifted from us burdens, dried our tears,
And "poured their balm on wounds" along the way.
Yes, "fallen on the road to Jericho,
And left for dead by robbers lain in wait,"
We've found their leader, Satan, as arch foe,
The chief of thieves, of murder, lust, and hate.
But though dire wounded, we revive in strength
To also aid those fallen in our days.
Then we before the throne shall come at length
To hear "Well done! You've won your Savior's praise!"
And He, our Savior, when those days are done,
Shall ever be World's Best "Samaritan!"

His "Home Sweet Home"

Perhaps you've heard about the man
Who sought his house to sell,
So went then to an agent
His intent there to tell.

He bade the man to advertise
In media what he had
Taken long for granted
As, simply said, his "pad."

The agent's ad enlargement
Portrayed the house as "grand."
It stunned the would-be seller
And caused a change in plan:

"Until I came to offer
For sale my property,
I didn't know I had so much!
But now its worth I see!"

"So, hey, I think I'll cancel
That offer I've made known;
'The pad' that I came here to sell
Is really 'Home Sweet Home!'"

Say, isn't that reaction
Like such from brains gone numb?
We don't know what God's giv'n "in store"
Until we've weighed their sum!

Gideon's Success and Sorrow
Judges 6 thru 8

"I'll be God's 'barley biscuit'
Sent rolling fast on track.
Though oh so weak, I'll risk it
To see God's foes laid flat!"

This Gideon's song, "Faith's Profit,"
When "Eavesdrop Camp" he fled,
Where God's most witless "prophet"
Proclaimed his own as dead.

O yes, a foe unknowing
Revealed a dream most odd,
Which meant his camp's o'erthrowing
And Gideon's "Go!" from God.

Indeed Manasseh's hero
Right then found God his stay.
With self decreased to zero,
It keyed his win that day.

With odds against his "army
(Preposterous, absurd!)
The foe was destroyed largely—
No more midst men was heard!

You've known, "If hopes were horses,
Indeed all bums would ride"?
But life's sad truth endorses
Oft times another side.

So after Gideon's conquest
"Fool's gold" became his god.
He fell with demons' onset
And Satan's forward nod!

Oh God, help today's heroes
To hold to faith, I ask;
The crown is with the credo
Of him who stays on task.

The Christian's Seven-Ups

1. WAKE UP! The sluggard will not rise from pleasant sleep,
   So poverty comes on him like a thief."
Proverbs 6:9-11: "How long will you slumber, O sluggard? When will you rise from your sleep?"

2. DRESS UP! It's good to look your best throughout your days,
   So "Put on Christ!" at dawn; live to His praise!
Romans 13:14:
"Put on the Lord Jesus Christ, and make no provision for the flesh, to fulfill its lusts."

3. SHUT UP! Our actions will at times be seen as worst;
   At dawn our shouting's taken as a curse!
Proverbs 27:14:
"He who blesses his friend with a loud voice, rising early in the morning, it will be taken as a curse from him!"

4. STAND UP! In times of lawlessness on every hand
   For truth and righteousness we all must stand!
Ephesians 6:14:
"Stand, therefore, having girded your waist with truth, having put on the breastplate of righteousness."

5. REACH UP! While men may faint in testing times through fear,
   It's then we know our God is very near.
Proverbs 3:5, 6:
"Trust in the Lord with all your heart, and lean not on your own understanding: In all your ways acknowledge Him, and He shall direct your paths."

6. PRAY UP! We must not let our lives be filled with care.
   When trials come we'll look to God in prayer.
Philippians 4:6, 7:
"Be anxious for nothing, but in everything by prayer and supplication, with thanksgiving, let your requests be made known to God."

7. LOOK UP! With troubles all about us we will sigh—
But know then Christ's appearing may be nigh!
*Luke 21:28: "...When all these things begin to come to pass,
then look up, and lift up your heads, for your redemption draws nigh!"*

How Could You Ever Hate Me So?!"

I saw the mask of terror on his face,
His body too convulse with fear!
The chains in pain he dragged with that doomed race
Toward final judgment as his fate drew near!

Oh no! That's Irvin Holden midst the damned—
My neighbor-friend of long ago!
Oh, then he cried to me in Heaven's land,
"HOW COULD YOU EVER HATE ME SO?!

"YOU FOUND THE SAVIOR WHO FOR ALL HAD BLED,
AND THEN WITH NONCHALANCE WENT ON YOUR WAY
WITH NONE OR LITTLE CARE FOR ME INSTEAD—
THE DAMNED AND HOPE DEVOID TODAY!!"

Oh, friend, do heed with me most prayerfully
Our lack of Spirit-fed desire
For those whose plight we ignore carelessly
Who daily face God's judgment fire!

These souls may well behold us hopelessly,
As Dives-like they view us in Heav'n's glow—
Then upward cry so copelessly,
"HOW COULD YOU EVER HATE ME SO?!"

It's true their fate they really can't disclaim
As looking elsewhere they excuse their tears—
But we could well find ISSUE FOR SOME BLAME,
THOUGH BRIEF, AS WE LOOK BACK ON CARELESS YEARS!

I Think That I Shall Never See

I think that I shall never see
Such differences 'twixt men and trees.

In fact with both viewed juxtaposed,
Men's sad corruptions are exposed:

The trees from God show they are blessed,
While men will question God exists!

From Providence the trees receive;
To chance alone men dare would cleave!

Trees' limbs are e'er upturned in praise,
But thankless men their curses raise!

The trees nest robins in their hair,
Men harbor fools, their shameful fare!

Upon the trees soft snow has lain;
Upon mankind there's only blame!

Our God is seen in ev'ry tree—
In men just sad depravity!

God's Gifts Given in John 3:16

Does God in Heaven sympathize
With us with cares so keen?
Well, we've in John chapter three no surprise
OF GREAT GIFTS GIVEN IN VERSE SIXTEEN!

He cared for us before we knew Him,
BEFORE CHRIST EVER CAME FROM THENCE.
His love's expressed so clearly for men—
IN "LOVED"—AS SEEN IN THE PAST TENSE!

And, O, the MAGNITUDE we know
Of love spelled out so great;
It's clearly seen in that word "SO,"
WHICH ONLY GOD COULD CONSUMMATE!

And WHO is meant to know such care,
For whom love's flag's unfurled?
Well, friend, it's championed everywhere—
AS "GOD SO LOVED THE WORLD"!

And, yes, this love is totally
About which we all should RAVE,
For it's revealed for you and me
AS THAT WHICH OUR GOD FREELY "GAVE"!

And what's the FULLNESS of this love,
This love for every one?
He gave in love sent from above
WITH CHRIST, "HIS ONLY SON"!

He gave Him that we might escape
Sin's PUNISHMENT so dire;
The wages due for us so great—
TO "PERISH" IN HELL FIRE!

Praise God, such wages we avoid!
But what's in their place so rife?
It's Heaven's good, e'en now enjoyed—
YES, EVEN "ETERNAL LIFE!"

An Addition to His "Home"
As originally built by Poet Edgar A. Guest

The poet said some livin's gotta go into a home.
And since that place ain't ready-made, ye've got to build on some.
He sez ye need some shadder with the love that warms the heart.
Ye need the young uns' laughter an' the old uns takin' part.
Ye need a lot o' elbow grease to make the thing t' go,
As well as lots o' huggin', friends, which melts the ice, you know.
But as another carpenter who's been aroun' awhile,
I'd here suggest an add-on room t'make our God t' smile.

O "It takes a heap o' livin' in a house t' make it home,"
But certainly we need the love o' Christ fer all who roam,
Who stray away from Mother's prayers an' from the Holy Word.
We need t' take our God as King, as Master, an' as Lord!
We need t' learn t' lean on Him Who died fer us one day,
T' trust Him through life's trials—an' then at last t' say:
"This house o' brick and mortar, from the cellar up t' dome,
At last in true reality, THIS HOUSE IS TRULY HOME!

God's Crazy 'Bout You!

If our God's got a "fridge," then your picture hangs on it,
And your photo as well could be there in His wallet.
He has sent you His sunshine and flowers each spring;
He's awakened His songbirds each morning to sing;
He has filled you quite full of His good things to eat;
And has deputized angels, each one your helpmeet.
Then of course in your trials, when bowed under cares,
Well, His ear has been open: He's answered your prayers.
God has healed your diseases through all of your years,
Given peace for your conflicts, dried a river of tears.

But the best is salvation, your soul's needs to mend;
Jesus died on Mt. Calv'ry to cancel your sins!
Though He could anywhere in this world make His throne,
He has crowned all by taking your heart as His home!
Now in short for the record, I'll say in review –
YOU ARE REALLY SOMBODY!
GOD'S CRAZY 'BOUT YOU!

My Christian Heart Is a Garden for Christ
"I have come to my garden, my sister, my spouse...." Song of Songs 5:1

The Christian's heart is a garden for Christ,
The Spirit of God avers.
It is considered of great price,
Confirmed in God's good Word.

I'd see it's kept for Christ alone;
No sharing with evil learned.
With ways of Satan here not known,
Love only is affirmed!

This garden shall be as fair can be;
All flowers to flourish in bloom.
The rarest of these you'll ever see,
Where blight of blame never comes.

Good growth you'll note in this garden here,
A growth profound 'mongst men.
It's through God's grace, which angels cheer
With growth ever upward toward Him.

I want my Lord to come in retreat—
After all, all His losses were mine.
And surely for Him all should now be replete
In things sanctified holy, divine.

No "Double Jeopardy"
1 Corinthians 15:3b; Acts 20:21, 22

Of all this sinner finds in God's Word
Especially one blesses me;
It's in assurance from my Lord
That there's no "double jeopardy!"

Oh, yes, one man has paid the cost
For all of man's misery;
That Man is Christ Who on His cross
Died for everyone's liberty!

But yet two needful things remain;
Without these one's still lost, I see:
Repentance and trust in Christ Heav'n obtains—
Otherwise there's still Hell's jeopardy

The Ruptured Reed and Smoking Flax

The ruptured reed Christ will not break
(I think sometimes that's I);
The smoking flax He'll not forsake
To burn away and die.

He calls us with our nagging needs
And fears that reflect shame.
He wants our trust though suff'ring much,
Our seeking Him in pain.

Tomorrow's lot with faith not lax
Well may not be as seen:
The ruptured reed and smoking flax
May reign His king and queen!

The "House" Known as Man
Inspired by Joyce Kilmer's "The House with Nobody In It"

I recall of a house once a home,
Sitting lone 'long "the Erie track,"
Looking sad, deserted, forlorn
For the need of the fam'ly it lacked;
That this house had its broken shutters,
And a yard overgrown with weeds;
It had sagging unpainted gutters,
And a roof falling in at the eaves!
So sad that its windows were broken,
That its vines needed trimming and tied—
But most grievous that this house betokened
The sore need of "a fam'ly inside!"

But beyond may we see here in type
That arch-typical "house" known as man,
Who once knew all the good things of life
With his God in that blest Eden's land!
There somehow with a greedy response
To his foe—so well-cloaked as his friend!—
He was robbed of The Good God ensconced
In his heart, and to what might have been!
Oh, so much like that poor house rehearsed,
   Sitting lone 'long "the Erie track,"
This sad "house" has reality's curse—
The dire need of the God that it lacks!

"They are all gone out of the way; they are together become
unprofitable;
THERE IS NONE THAT DOETH GOOD, NO NOT EVEN ONE!"
—ROMANS 3:12

"Our God Is In the Gale!"
2 Samuel 5:24, 25; Acts 2:1-4a, 47

King David said, "Men, you should know
   When rustling's in the trees
It's time to rise to fight our foes;
   Our God is in the breeze!

"Now winds are blowing!
O, let's get going!
God's ventures will prevail!
The Spirit's moving,
Our strength renewing—
Our God is in the gale!"

O, then it was from strength depleted
   Roused soldiers knew a rout;
The enemy indeed defeated,
   From Israel was cast out.

Since that event at Pentecost
There came a mighty wind,
With God reclaiming sinners lost,
The devil's deeds to end!

And times are still propitious now—
Not time to pout and pine!
With Spirit pow'r meant for this hour
See God work in our times!

Yes, "Winds are blowing,
O let's get going!
God's ventures will prevail!
The Spirit's moving,
Our strength renewing—
Our God is in the gale!"

"Sahara-like," We Need Renewal

Both God's way and His will in the Bible
Are so clearly set forth for our good.
To neglect these indeed makes us li'ble
To shame Him and ourselves, understood.

As we need nourishment for our body,
For our spirit the same is the case.
Without such normal needs everybody
Will but die, fail to win in life's race.

Without life-giving rain whatsoever—
That's no place we would be, I can state;
And we know such a place, named Sahara,
To which none without help here could face.

Now the rain coming down, God's Word speaking,
Says to us it's that Word that we need.
So when we in self-will, God not heeding,
Like Sahara we're left as to deeds!

And, likewise, without prayer life is futile—
If not worse we become too at length!
Yes, indeed, we could even turn brutal—
Surely fruitless, at least, in our strength.

So may daily we come to our Maker
For renewal in life to be true.
Through God's Word and our prayers we're partakers
Of God's best—NO "SAHARA" IN VIEW!

"The saddest words in tongue or pen
are the sad, sad words, 'It might have been!'"
—author unknown

Since Escaping I Would Flee!

Oh, yes, through Christ I have escaped
God's judgment on my sin,
But vestiges of its pow'r remains
To plague me from within.

The Spirit says there's needful flight
If fruitful here I'd be.
O, Lord, help me in Jesus' name
That I indeed shall flee!

I do not want to reach Your throne
Without life's vict'ries won.
How I would hate to hang my head
With shame with life's work done!

May all sin's lusts and greediness
Be trophies of God's grace.
I would lay such at Jesus' feet
When I shall see His Face!

No "wood nor hay nor stubble," Lord,
Be mine there to behold.
I would cast at Those Pierced Feet
My crowns of purest gold!

2 Peter 1:4; 2 Tim. 2:22; 1 Cor. 3:12; Rev. 4:10, 11.

I Do Desire Your Fullness, Lord!
In memory of Samuel Morris, 1872-1893

At one time or another all have feelings that we're left
Alone to face uncertainties. Indeed we've felt bereft
With no one as our helper versus hurts perceived and real.
The trauma of such thought is often hard to heal.

Christ Jesus knew that He must leave for service at God's throne,
So told His church while gone away they'd not be left alone.
He'd send Another Comforter, Another like Himself.
This One would bless them as none could, their All Sufficient Help.

And so in pow'r at Pentecost The Spirit of the Lord
Descended as God's Gracious Gift, fulfilling Jesus' word.
And now it's true all "born again" do have this Comforter
To aid us in our work for Christ and help us feel secure.

O Blessed Holy Spirit, here do help me in my quest.
I want to know Christ better while I live a life that's best.
Like Samuel Morris, Lord, from jungles once had come,
I do desire Your fullness, Lord, to bless men in The Son!

Against Those Savage Situations

Against those savage situations
Which cause our souls to seethe,
We've found our Savior's admonitions
Have served sweet ends in peace.

Yes, when "beside ourselves" so sore,
So set in our distresses,
We've found our God to be the more
Our Helper here to bless us.

So come, Sweet Savior, now to help us;
Yes, come for ev'ry hour.
O come with sacred salves to heal us
And strength to serve with power.

On Burying Grudges—Not Bearing Them
James 1:18-20; James chapters 3 & 4

We all could share those times as such
When unkind words we've known.
These oft produce the worst in us,
   To which our hearts are prone!

Yes, we are prone to bearing hate
Toward our own brotherhood.
This harb'ring we can't vindicate;
   It devastates all good!

Full many a church has shut its doors
When Satan had his way.
Where hurtful words are not abhorred
   Church fights come into play!

No, we can't pray when there's ill will
Toward any of God's own.
Its poison chills, our hearts will fill,
   If not forgiv'n, atoned!

I'm sure it also shortens lives
As "suicide by stealth."
It's harmed our children, hurt our wives,
   And eaten up our wealth!

How foolish then to BEAR a grudge!
Much better far 'twould be
If we before Our God, The Judge,
   Would BURY THEM, you see!

God, Give Us YOUR Enough!
"…Esau said, 'I have enough, my brother….' And Jacob said, 'I also have enough…..'"—Genesis 33:13-15

Perhaps it's true we've heard the word,
"For life, Lord, fill my cup."
And yet in truth folks rarely find
They ever GET enough!

A rarity in olden times
Two patriarchs confessed
That God had given them much good;
They both were fully blessed.

But little did they realize
That God had more in store
Of what we would call "GOOD AND BAD"—
And BOTH WERE NEEDED MORE.

Example: Jacob in life's course
Would find great JOY AND GRIEF;
And later then in truth averred,
"GOD'S MADE MY LIFE COMPLETE!"

A lesson then from him let's learn:
The wisdom from above
Knows that we need both "GOOD AND BAD,"
Which God supplies in love.

There's a Difference

I would not work to enter Heaven,
For Christ the work has done;
But I would work sun-up to seven
For love of Christ, God's Son!
Ephesians 2:8-10

He said, "We Shall Go Over!"
Matthew 14:15-33

In the Gospels we read how our Lord in great power
    Manifested His mercy with souls whom He'd feed.
Some five thousand had fed on His Word, but an hour
    Saw one other hunger develop in need.

And, you know, our dear Lord looked upon all those faces
    With sympathy too for new food that they pled.
So He took a lad's lunch and with action most gracious
    Did grow that small portion so all were there fed!

O, thank God for the fact they enjoyed a great blessing—
    Super-ample it was! But Christ saw a third need:
He therefore once more spoke with disciples' need pressing,
    "Now this sea we'll go over!" New needs thus they'd heed.

And, I say, here take note: He said, "We shall go over"—
    They'd go over that water—not under the sea!
Yes, His simple word was with omnipotent power;
    Indeed, they'd "go over"—a fiat, decree!

Yet how sad midst the tempest they shortly encountered
    Those twelve had great fear, that in truth they'd be killed!
They cried, "Lord, here we'll drown! This boat surely will founder!"
    But then hear His sure word, "I say, storm, you be still!"

And, my friends, in life's trials we're likewise sore tested.
    We all come to the times when we think all is lost!
But our Lord, always with us, will not see us bested—
Like those twelve "We'll go over" life's waves though storm tossed!

An Example in Candy our Cat

A cat that was spayed once was saved from sad fate
    —She deemed feral through losing her home—
Where the thunder storms raked, seeming so animate,
    Even pelting her quite to the bone!

So my son and his wife became saviors, as when
They provided her help at their door;
Just a warm little nest gave to this cat some rest –
But just minimal comfort, no more.

Yes our Candy – so named – was withheld from the best
(With an allergy named there to blame)
Till we two as on quest, yes, a couple God-blest,
Came suggesting THEIR home as their aim.

So set on a new plane to The Sun State she came –
That's OUR Candy to thrive, all would vouch.
Yet when storms would o'er take to a refuge she'd race –
That's the safe underside of our couch!

Oh a refuge in Christ I would here now address
With our cat as example, you know—
Yes, her action attests and her haven suggests
As to how and to Whom WE should go.

Friends, when fears would distress and cares cause upset
It's to Christ we must hasten for sure!
He's our Haven 'gainst threat, and where foes we forget,
And where snug and in peace WE endure!

Yes, from Candy our cat, and her haven all that
We've been taught here as humans indeed
That from Heav'n's habitat Christ can care for a cat—
And for sinners like us in dire need.

"Thus Far the Lord Has Helped Us"
1 Samuel 7:12

"Thus far the Lord has helped us,
Our witness through the years.
There in our yesterdays
He's calmed our faithless fears,
Forgiven wayward wand'ring,
And dried our tardy tears.

"Thus far the Lord has helped us,"
Still holds for each today.
He is "The Same forever"
To hear us when we pray;
Especially in trials,
We look to Him, our Stay.

"Thus far the Lord has helped us"
With courage to pursue
Our hopes for each tomorrow
As faithful still and true.
Yes, for dark days that lie ahead
He'll be our Helper too!

Hey, I'm Loaded on John 3:16!

As a boozer I'd truly had troubles;
To the devil I'd paid some big dues!
Oh, my home life, it lay in sins' rubble!
Woe was me, I had alcohol blues!

But I've had that big belt from the Bible!
One good draught from God's Word made me clean!
Now for boozin' I'm no longer li'ble—
Hey, I'm loaded on John 3:16!

Now my new life is set on full throttle,
And, praise Jesus, I've learned from God's Word
That true peace can't be bought in a bottle—
Now that thought's absolutely absurd!

Yes, I've had that big belt from the Bible!
One good draught from God's Word made me clean!
Now for boozin' I'm no longer li'ble—
Hey, I'm loaded on John 3:16!

But praise God there's still one Fluid flowin'—
Like Cana's wine it's also crimson red;
It's our Lord's Precious Blood, and I'm knowin'
That it cleanses from sin, like He said!

Praise God for that belt from the Bible!
Oh that draught from God's Word made me clean!
Now for boozin' I'm no longer li'ble—
Yes, I'm loaded on John 3:16!

And right now I will pledge to you, Father,
When someone comes suggestin' a toast,
That I'll say, "Please just give me some water—
For God's filled me with His Holy Ghost!"

Oh, bless God for that belt from the Bible!
For that draught from God's Word made me clean!
Now for boozin' I'm no longer li'ble—
Thank God I'm loaded on John 3:16!

Hey, brother, are YOU loaded on John 3:16?

CHAPTER THREE: POEMS ON THE TONGUE, PRAYER AND PRAISE

Thank God for the fact that He has given his church the gift of prayer and praise for His and this world's benefits! Praise Him that the perhaps smallest member of our bodies, the tongue, can be so used for both ours and others' eternal good; and I hope that you, my readers of these poems, are so using your tongues today! I no doubt would be the world's worst liar to state I have always used mine for God's and mankind's benefits—but I am endeavoring to improve in my efforts to grow in this grace with God's help.

Unfortunately, friends, the Bible in several places, but in the epistle of James especially, teaches that the tongue can also be a member of the body used with the greatest of blame. Only eternity will reveal the hurt this little member—like carelessly attended fires in a forest!—has caused through the years! I have sought to emphasize the hurt that can be in our tongues in the poems that follow.

Also, however, to counterbalance the negatives on the subject of the tongue I have also included here several poems on prayer—a practice that I have widely espoused but sadly admit that I have not practiced as I should have. I here also lift up the praise which our Lord in Psalm 22:3 tells us He "inhabits" or "sits enthroned upon." This reference in the Psalms is an obvious indication that our God has high standards for the use of that little member from the faithful. Indeed throughout the word of God we are encouraged to give praise and thanksgiving continually to our God, as well as in prayer to Him. In this section of my book I pray such wholesome practices will be advanced to God's glory. Pray with me also, won't you?

I'll Praise My God Forever
"Thanks be to God for His indescribable Gift!"—1 Cor. 2:9 NKJV

A woman wrote a book in which she tried to tout
A list of "fourteen thousand things" one may be glad about.
She didn't give God credit, was lacking there in praise—
'Twas missing in her thanks of Him Who surely crowns men's days!

In contrast our Late pastor, through whom our church had thrived,
Asked all to list one hundred gifts of God seen in their lives.
So I would take my pen up now to praise in poetry
This One Whom I'm indebted to, Who's blessed me wondrously.

I praise my God for mercy; I praise my God for grace;
I praise my Lord Who shed His Blood my dark sins to erase.
I praise my God, all sovereign, Who works up there above,
Inspiring me toward holiness and deeds of selfless love.

I praise Christ for His Spirit, The One like to my Lord,
Who's given us to serve and laud as One always Adored;
I praise God for my Bible, the Holy Word so true—
My life in its totality so blest, by it renewed.

I praise God for "The Bridegroom" (I take my place as "bride")
That here with His sweet Person I've strength now to abide.
I praise God for my trials, that though they seem dire tests,
I know that in God's alchemy they'll turn out for the best.

I praise God for my calling and gifts to speak and write.
I feel through these I honor Him—though poems may seem trite!
I'm hopeful for my future, firm fixed upon God's Word,
Which tells of God's tomorrows as being most superb.

But now I think I'll pause a bit, reflecting here in time
Upon one hundred blessings which in sum make life to rhyme.
In fact, Paul the Apostle in speaking of them all,
Says it's indeed impossible that we could all recall:

"Our eyes have never seen, nor ears could hear the sum
Of gifts our God has given us until His kingdom comes."
But here's one Gift in summary which tells all in a word:
I'll praise my God forever for Christ my Living Lord!

Praise The Son Light! Praise Our God!
"I am The Light of the World!"—Jesus, John 8:12

At the dawning of Earth's day
Christ proclaimed, "Let there be light!"
And then promptly fled away
All vestiges of night!

Then the courts of Heaven rang;
How the blessed angels sang!
Singing, "Glory! Glory! Glory!
Give man's Savior all the laud!"
Singing, "Glory! Glory! Glory!
Praise The Son Light! Praise Our God!"

What a wondrous day had dawned
On one Calvary's dark scene,
When The Son Light smiled upon
This sad world to intervene!

Then the courts of Heaven rang;
How the blessed saints all sang!
Singing, "Glory! Glory! Glory!
Give Our Savior all the laud!"
Singing, "Glory! Glory! Glory!
Praise The Son Light! Praise Our God!"

O what blessing does unfold
When Christ's peace first fills the heart;
When The Son breaks on the soul
Our salvation to impart!

Then the courts of Heaven ring!
How the blessed saints all sing!
Singing, "Glory! Glory! Glory!
Give Our Savior all the laud!"
Singing, "Glory! Glory! Glory!
Praise The Son Light! Praise Our God!"

Praise Is the Primer for Prayer
Psalm 50:23

Praise is the primer that primes up the pump
Of provision God loves to provide.
Yes, if we'd be appraising some prize from His sump,
Then we'll pray with the praise He prescribes.

Perfected Praise
Job 38:7; 1 Chron. 16:4-7; Acts 16:25; Eph. 5:19; Rev. 5:8,9

Creation days saw anthems raised
As God was lifted high.
The morning Stars sang forth in praise
With none to breathe doubt's sigh.

Our God conveyed that temple days
Should see His songs be sung.
And Paul displayed the self-same ways,
Urged praise upon each tongue.

In this church age there's endless praise
That's heard the world around.
Off great highways and down byways
Paeans of praise resound.

Now my tongue's praise to God I'll raise
Till finished are my tasks
When heav'nly days shall see all praise
Perfected there at last.

My Prayer

"...Let us continually offer the sacrifice of praise to God...."
—Heb. 13:15.

Dear Lord, I'd not go moaning, groaning
Along life's sometimes weary road,
For such succeeds to sin's sad scorning
Of Heaven's very best, I know.
Instead with hopes for my tomorrows,
I'll praise you, Lord, each step I've trod,
Till winning vict'ry o'er my sorrows
I've found sweet rest at home with God.
This my prayer in Jesus' name.

I Pray for Grace Again

"It is God Who works within you both to will and to do of His good pleasure."—Phil. 2:13

O Lord today in many ways
I've been so prone to sin,
And now abed I pillow my head
Upon your grace again!
And, yes, O Lord, I trust Your word
That cleansed I'm safe, secure;
That there's no doubt I'm not cast out—
That Your love still endures!

As You concur I here aver
Tomorrow's race I'll run,
And, yes, I'll win o'er self and sin
In pledge of Heaven to come!

The Way Is Raised!
John 14:6; Galatians 6:14a

The little birds in symphony
Help dawn light up the day,
While daffodils in harmony
Add essence to their lay.

Yet why, oh why, with muted mouth—
Or worse with curses vile!—
Creation's greatest groan in drought
Nor gives God praise the while?

An awful tale that must be told—
Told sadly to all nations:
Man gave up God for gods most cold—
And icy isolation!

But oh my God, is there no hope,
No claim to reclamation?
Must we go on as now to grope
And dwell in fell stagnation?

NO, GOD BE PRAISED, THE WAY IS RAISED
TO SALVAGE MAN SO LOST!
BELIEVE TODAY, AND SEE, I SAY,
SALVATION IN CHRIST ON HIS CROSS!

Prayer Principles

The disciples of Christ SOUGHT IT.
"Lord, teach us to pray."—Lk. 11:1;
Therefore our Lord Jesus TAUGHT IT.
"After this manner you should pray...."—Matt. 6:9.
And so today we have the OUGHT OF IT.
"Men ought always to pray, and not to faint!"—Lk. 18:1.
God's Righteousness was WROUGHT BY IT.
"Through faith (believers) wrought righteousness..."—Heb. 11:33.
In trouble Daniel was FRAUGHT BY IT.
"Whoever prays to any but you...shall be cast to the lions!"—Dan. 6:7.

For its power one would have BOUGHT IT.
"...Money perish with you who thought to buy the gift of God!"
—Acts 8:20.
Too late the rich man BESOUGHT BY IT.
"Send Lazarus to touch my tongue with a drop of water!"—Luke 16:14.
Hard hearts will gain NOUGHT BY IT.
"...Forgive not?...neither will your Father forgive you"—Matt. 6:15.
The Spirit's help is BROUGHT BY IT.
"The Holy Spirit makes intercession with groanings."—Rom. 8:26.
At last Samuel believing CAUGHT IT.
"If He calls to you again, pray, 'Speak Lord!'"—1 Sam. 3:10.
In wrestling, Jacob FOUGHT BY IT.
"I will not let you go unless you bless me."—Gen. 32:26.
Ahaz would have NOUGHT OF IT.
"I will not ask nor test...the Lord."—Isaiah 7:12.

Thank God for Prayers Unanswered!
1 Kings 19

Thank God for prayers unanswered!
We sometimes must exclaim.
Petitions on self centered
Don't win, the fact is plain.
Yes, prayer-time can be squandered
When such are prayed in vain.

Elijah was a prophet
Pursued by Jezebel,
Who saw in life no profit
But chose on death to dwell—
To him a helpful topic
Compared then to his "hell!"

This man wished life aborted,
That from it he'd find rest;
Yes, death indeed he courted
From God with earnest breath.
But it is unrecorded—
AS YET HE'S **NOT** SEEN DEATH!

Oh may we, our God praising,
Be glad when prayers don't win.
Instead let's praise be raising
When God says "No," to men.
This fact may seem amazing—
SOME PRAYERS HAVE SENSE OF SIN!

Hurricane Katrina and Hope through Prayer

I'd hoped this year that we'd be spared God's fury,
   That He instead would grant His gracious love;
But, oh, I know that wrath reserved is surely
   What we in sin deserve from God above.
We've scorned His Word, His prophets' warnings;
   And still we're fully set in our sad sins.
We've seemingly lost semblances of moorings,
   And horror haunts our house without, within!

Infanticide is married to our mis'ry,
   Perversions' sexualities are viewed!
Our schools have relegated God to hist'ry
   With prayer provisions proscribed too!
Can we expect past hist'ry's God of Mercy
   To lend a list'ning ear now to our cries?
We know He has real controversy
   With nations chained as we to idol ties!

But we still hope in God as did past remnants,
   Who like undaunted Daniel sighed for sins.
Or like Habakkuk with great faith attendant
Said through our chast'ning we'll still hope in Him.
   And like the psalmist we in silence wait
   With firm assurance that our God still cares;
That He'll provide though mountains flee away,
   For being God He yet hears humble prayers!

November Reflections
Luke 17:12-19; Romans 1:18,32; Galatians 6:14

On this November day we're expressing
Thanksgiving to God, ever near us.
It is true we have known His real blessings;
With great needs in our lives they have cheered us.

God forbid we should be as those nine
Who of ten cured of leprosy went
On their way—but with thanks not inclined!
Only ONE had true praiseful intent!

And such lack of love's gratitude means
One may well know its sure devastation;
For God's Word indeed tells such demeans
Both ourselves and our God of creation.

Let's declare with our lips love's emotion,
Thanking God for His most common blessings:
Air we breathe, foods we eat, mates' devotion—
Yes, with healings, our doctors assessing.

But, beyond, we are glad for the dearest:
We give thanks for God's most gracious love,
Christ's advent, His dire death, and Blest Spirit,
Our new life, Himself waiting above.

He Prays the Best Who loves the Best

It's true I'd reprimanded him,
My Billy at his play.
The need for rain had left me grim,
Just "out of sorts," I'd say.

You see, he'd turned the sprinklers on
To splash about in fun.
He couldn't share my care upon
The drought which left all numb.

So I explained about our farm,
How thirsting things can die;
How water surely saves from harm,
So saving it we'll try.

When later at my sink I stood
I saw my boy move past
So carefully into our woods
A cup held in some task.

When he came out and then returned
I saw that cup still gripped,
And knew with water Billy yearned
Some thirsting thing to lift.

The third time then I followed him
To find attention drawn
Upon a shape in front of him—
There lay a sickened fawn!

And Billy now was so intent
On giving it to drink,
While praying loud in innocence,
As each child would, I think.

Oh our great land in such dire straits,
With drought some sure to die!
And viewing this my heart did ache
As tears welled in my eyes.

And mercifully from out that grove
It then began to rain.
I felt the love of God He showed
Where Billy shared the pain.

And this I know, "One prays the best
Who loves...," And God could tell
That surely Billy met this test
In prayer where one fawn fell.

"On Hanging Harps on Willow Trees"

From research of the facts it's been shown
That the willow has always been known
As the symbol of weeping, yes, of tears,
And no doubt such shall be through the years.

As to "Hanging of harps on willow trees,"
Such goes back far into history,
To sad stories of Jews' chastening
While in bondage and called on to sing.

There they said that they could not rejoice,
That for gaiety they had no voice;
That their harps, emblems of victory,
Must be hung there on sad willow trees.

And it's true in this day for God's own,
We oft times too are caused here to groan.
Then for sorrow we cry through nights long,
Because sin so deprives us of song.

Yet praise God we have Scriptural light
Which we hold to in "chast'ning's dark night":
Though our harps on the willow will swing,
Sins forgiven we take them and sing!

Our Lord Once Worked a Work for Men
"All are under sin...whose mouth is full of cursing and bitterness."—
Rom. 3:9, 14

Men's cursing comes forth naturally,
Like weeds sprout from the ground.
But roses require work, you see,
Before sweet scents surround.
And so our Lord with God's accord
Once worked a work for men;
Upon His cross He took our loss,
Sin's cursing to amend.
Such disgrace traced to Adam's race

Benumbs each tribe and nation,
While praises prove we've found God's love,
Are born Christ's new creation.

That Boneless Tongue!
James 3:3-12

That boneless tongue unlike our arm
Can far outstrip it doing harm!
Just turn it loose with hurtful word,
It can destroy more than a sword!

As for offenders, wisdom saith,
It oft portends one's early death!
Though giv'n for good, in woe instead
Sometimes it says, "Man's lost his head!"

Christ's brother, James, so learned it well:
"The tongue oft times spawns fires of hell!
Yes, like a match, so potent, dire,
If can out-flame a forest fire!"

Let sinners all now hear my song:
Oh God, do guard my tongue from wrong!

On "Laying Isaac Down"

"Friend Abraham, your serving Me
So far has been profound;
But now I ask more sacrifice—
You must 'lay Isaac down.'

"Oh, God, did I hear what You said?
Your word to me confounds!
How could I view my Isaac dead,
In sacrifice 'laid down?'

"He's been our miracle conceived;
By old age we've been bound—
And now you say of him received,
We must 'lay Isaac down'?!"

"Yes, yours, my son, is to obey;
Let faith your life surround.
He Who has blessed you till today
Now says, Lay Isaac down!"

"But, Lord, how could You thus be praised,
Your name held in renown?
What of the promises You've made,
With Isaac thus 'laid down'?"

"Your questions, son, do not enhance
Your faith till now so sound.
My purposes, though they confuse,
Prevail—Lay Isaac down!"

Friends, Abaham eternally
Is hailed this world around,
For Isaac in a figure see
RAISED UP WHOM HE 'LAID DOWN'!

"By faith Abraham...offered up Isaac, and he who had received
the promises, offered up his only begotten son, of whom
it was said, 'In Isaac your seed shall be called,' con-
cluding that God was able to raise him up,
even from the dead, from which he
received him in a figure."
Hebrews 11:17

God's Lessons in the Bees

Lord, I'd be like the honey bees
Who live their lives as one.
Yes, harmony means unity
Where selfishness is shunned.

No bee is seen to contravene
The will of all displayed.
God made them thus harmonious
To give each other aid.

The worker bees most vig'rously
Serve all with one accord.
The queen? Well, she is sov'reign, see;
So Christians hold their Lord.

As equals known so are the drones;
They simply sire the young.
A jelly made through flowers' trade
Gives strength to get things done.

Another matter I'd explore
So taught to us by bees,
Lies in the lore that we abhor—
Invasion, as do these!

Yes, they'll attack —no sting held back —
When any come to test.
As JEWS, my friend, WE'LL surely fend
Off foes to guard OUR nest!

So summing up the lessons learned
From these, our insect friends:
We do affirm that we will yearn
Our mutual good to blend;

We'll include dues for "drones" less used
While hon'ring God our King;
We'll guard with zest—give foes no rest
Who to us harm would bring!

Let's Bloom Where We've Been Planted

My local church in Jacksonville
Where Gospel truth is found
Stayed put when they were tempted
To seek "more gracious grounds."

The urban rot around them,
More evident each year,
Had caused some folk to option
The world's ways to adhere:

To take up flight to suburbs
Where weren't those awful smells,
The sights, the sounds occurring
Which caused some to repel.

But most have sung this chorus,
A word of wisdom true
Full based upon God's dictum
Our home-call to pursue:

"Let's bloom where we've been planted,
Light candles in the night,
Observe the word reliant
To bless where there is blight."

O yes, this comes from Jesus,
Who is our Greatest Fan;
He wants us for His witness,
Gives gifts so that we can

'...You shall be witnesses unto me, both in Jerusalem, and in all Judea, and in Samaria, and unto the uttermost part of the earth."—Acts 1:8b

The Night-blooming Cereus
"My help comes from the Lord...He Who keeps Israel will not slumber...nor sleep." —Psa. 121:3;
"...In the night His song shall be with me."—Psa. 42:8

The night-blooming cereus points up the fact
That our God works in nature, His purpose exact,
Illustrating His power on this earthly ball,
Bringing praise to His Person and power withal.

Yes, consider the truth, when the sun's rays are gone
Which cause flowers to bloom, it then saddens men's song.
Nonetheless see these buds op'ning up with no light,
Therein proving God's there and prevails in the night.

As the lesser is true, so the greater also:
Weak one, God isn't dead, though some might think Him so!
O He never has slumbered—be instant in prayer—
Though your night may be dark, still your God surely cares!

And great blessings yet blossom for you from above—
It's the lesson the cereus sends of God's love!
So away then with doubting: THOUGH DARK BE YOUR NIGHT,
GOD'S PRESENCE GIVES RISE
TO THE PRAISE OF HIS MIGHT!

CHAPTER FOUR: POEMS RELATED TO PROPHECY, ESPECIALLY TO THE CHURCH AND NATION OF ISRAEL.

My dear mother, long deceased now, had a great interest in Bible prophecy, and she communicated that interest to me also, as indicated in the following I believe. Yes, I think God has great things in store for His church, and for the people of Israel too in the future! I'm surely trusting that soon we'll begin to see the reality of this, as His will is made known with great power in the world!

For the church God's will indeed will be made known soon, I hope and pray, in the Rapture, or His calling the church out of this world. Signs seem to increase to give all Christians hope.

Also, friends, I believe the stage is being set in history for Israel as a nation to trust in the Christ they have so long ignored, this both corporately and personally. Someone has said, "Keep your eyes on Palestine! Here the future of the world will soon be revealed for all to see!" And aren't events of a seemingly significant nature being revealed daily as I write? I surely think so.

An incident was recently made known to me which particularly piqued my interest particularly for that small nation's prophetic future. An aged man, well over 100 in years and so respected by people of his native land, was about to die, and he said he would leave a document with his passing which should not be opened and read until his death—which would reveal, said he, Whom he believed to be Israel's true Messiah. Upon his death, this document was opened eagerly and read, and it revealed: "JESUS OF NAZARETH, SO LONG REJECTED BY US, IS INDEED OUR TRUE MESSIAH"! Oh, God grant that this beleaguered people will soon come to know this One Whom I so love and the world so needs! What a future in blessing individually and nationally all shall then have!

"The Rapture" in "The Revelation"
John 14:3; Rev. 1:19; 1 Thess. 4:14-17; Rev. 3:10; 1 Thess. 5:9

When Christ returns again to earth
His church shall first arise.
This is "The Rapture" as Paul shows,
Our calling to the skies.

Yes, Christ indeed will come again
To reign, God's faithful know,
But is there some precise time frame
That Holy Scriptures show?

O yes, I see a sure sequence
In "The Revelation" shown,
Where found in chapter one, nineteen
Is its key verse, I own.

Here first there's reference to our Lord,
Seen viewed most gloriously;
Then "things which are" in this church age,
These seen sequentially.

Yes, seven churches are revealed,
Prophetic in the whole;
So perfect seven to us speaks;
And these past hist'ry hold.

Church age complete, John is called out—
Which action is abrupt—
And so "The Rapture of the church,"
With saints in joy caught up.

From chapter four then to nineteen,
The church to Heav'n conveyed
Is surely not on earth here seen
Till nineteen's judgment day.

Instead, in four, around God's throne
Are "elders," reports John,
With these saints in the Greek there shown
As "presbuterion."

Counterparts in church hist'ry
Became of well known fame,
But here I think they represent
All saints by our Lord claimed!

Succeeding chapters reveal "wrath"
By mortals never dreamt—
But is there not some most clear verse
To show the church exempt?

Praise God, there is in chapter three,
Verse ten that shows them spared
From "testing" coming on the earth—
Because God's word they'd shared!

Now, finally, a word from Paul
Concerns this "wrath to fall";
To Thessalonians he says
The church avoids it all.

I cannot let this poem pass—
With perhaps billions "lost"—
Except I say, IN CHRIST YOU'RE SAFE
BECAUSE HE BORE SIN'S COSTS!"

Just Where Are We in Prophecy?

Just where are we in prophecy?
So many want to know.
With latest twists in history
I'd here my viewpoint show:

Both Christians and the Jews in type
Are viewed in "Egypt's land"
With "Savior Joseph" and our Christ,
Redeemer of all men.

When Joseph died, in time arose
A stranger to His God,
Who killed their children, as he chose,
"The god of force" to laud.

With passing time Jews' seers foretold
Deliv'rance was in view;
But pharaoh angered and more bold
Afflicted Jews anew.

Great tribulation then God sent
All over Egypt's land,
And in the end for Jews it meant
Salvation per God's plan!

Oh yes, the Christians still are there,
With Christian Jews in blame.
And tribulation there they share
Who see their Lord defamed.

Yes, Christians now as one with Jews
Endure dread Satan's hate.
But we'll be saved—proclaim the news!
Who for God's kingdom wait!

A Lesson from "Hurricane Charley"

A hurricane named "Charley"
Did blot out Friday's sun;
And as it roared up toward us
We asked, "Has our time come?"

If experts' dire predictions
Were right, it couldn't miss;
At least we'd know some losses
When here our homes were hit.

So, yes, we prayed for blessing
And asked if God be pleased
That we'd be spared storm's fury,
His mercy we'd receive.

Our eyes transfixed with worry
Saw it turn before their plan.
It came ashore south of us,
While some were near unmanned!

And, oh, what devastations!
What hell in that storm's path!
What havoc, what great losses—
Oh, spare us yet its wrath!

It moved then northward toward us—
But then turned out to sea!
Praise God, it skirted 'round us!
Its anger we'd not see!

Oh, then what exclamations
Of joy were wafted here!
What praise, oh, what thanks giving!—
God heard our anxious prayer!

But are those then great sinners
Upon whom horrors fell?
Indeed, did God in fury
Send on them our storm's hell?

Oh, no we should not judge them;
Calamities are meant
To warn all unrepentant
Of Hell yet to be sent!

Luke 13:3-5—"There were present at that season some who told Jesus about the Galileans whose blood Pilate had mingled with their sacrifices. And Jesus answered and said to them: `Do you suppose that these Galileans were worse sinners than all other Galileans, because they suffered such things? I tell you, no; but unless you repent you will all likewise perish. Or those eighteen on whom The Tower of Siloam fell and killed them, do you think they were worse sinners than all other men who dwelt in Jerusalem? I tell you, no, but unless you repent, you will all likewise perish."

When "Swords to Ploughshares" Come to Be

The God who notes the sparrow's fall,
Charts their kind through the air,
Is God of all, hears when we call
On Him in sincere prayer.

So as this old year runs its course
And soldiers' carnage keep,
Oh that we'll make God our Resource
For everlasting peace!

Believe me, friends, we'll one day see—
According to The Book—
Our "swords to ploughshares" come to be
And "spears to pruning hooks."

And yet, dear friends, what happiness
Now each of us can own!
What now is ours in heavenly bliss
With Christ in hearts enthroned!

We'll one day wake, see for Christ's sake,
The world's sins nullified—
That's when by faith MANKIND SHALL TAKE
HIM AS THEIR KING WHO DIED!

Israel in the Cross Hairs
Gen. 12:3; Lk. 21:24b; Matt. 24:22

Pell-mell the nations move toward hell,
Ill omens all about,
As they for Israel sound death's knell,
Whose state they would "wipe out!"

And, friends, this poet is concerned
With gloom so looming 'round.
Brave people's hopes are overturned;
Despair, unchecked, abounds!

Rogue nations make their atom bombs,
While treasuries go bust;
Justice from the courts absconds,
And Israel must adjust!

Yes, fate with steady tread moves on,
And hate relays her costs.
Mark Israel now as "woebegone"—
But touch her at your loss!

Bad years converge which must cut short,
"Else no flesh would be saved!"
Except sin's carnage God aborts,
The world fills up its grave!

But Israel with the best yet known
Shall find her all in all.
Her faithfulness shall be enthroned
As she before Christ falls!

I pray the U.S., long foresworn
To guard brave Israel's place,
Shall in this day not yield to scorn
And so forfeit God's grace!

God's Proven Providences
Genesis 21:8a; Ezekiel 37:1-14; Genesis 12:3

Relating to God's providence
For some becomes a task,
But I'll expound it with great joy,
As you, I hope, would ask

A promise made to Abraham
Concerning his offspring
Has come to pass in mideast lands,
In Jews' awakening!

For two millennium almost
She's slept as just "dry bones,"
But now raised up as a great host
She lives, by her God owned!

And perhaps soon, we'd dare project—
God's Word in full accord—
She'll stand full roused, yes we expect,
Embracing Christ her Lord!

And oh the glory such bespeaks
When Israel, in God's grace,
Rejoices in The One Men Seek,
Full blest to lead our race!

But, viewing now the other side
Of providences known,
All nations versus Jews allied
Have fallen, damned, disowned!

Oh may our land, the U.S.A.,
Not drift from our great past
When we as Israel's friend always
Knew blessings unsurpassed!

Yet here so sadly I relate
That some—most foolishly!—
Renounce the Jewish ship of state
As enemies, I see!

If that position we pursue
Against God's clear-taught Word,
Our foolishness we'll live to rue
Forsaken, damned, abhorred.

Dread Armageddon Looms!

"Kiss the Son, lest He be angry, and you perish from the way when His wrath is kindled but a little!"—Psalm 2:12.

God's winds of war are blowing;
'Gainst all His foes they're hurled;
His holiness full-showing,
These lie in greatest peril!
But hounds of hell, resistant,
Have too cast off reserve,
Especially persistent
'Gainst all in Christ preserved!

Yet we have seen God's standard
Lifted o'er the tide.
Our Righteous Ruler, angered,
Will not hell's hate abide!
He's marshaled heaven's forces,
For Armageddon's strife
And will with His resources
Defeat His foes with might!

To those not yet preserved thus,
From judgment's awful flood
Redemption's in Christ Jesus,
Full paid with His own Blood!

But, oh, if you're resistant,
Dread Armageddon looms;
You've no one to embrace then
But Satan and his doom!

"...The devil that deceived them was cast into the Lake of Fire...
And whoever was not found written in the Book of
Life was cast into The Lake of Fire, this is
The second death."—Revelation 20:10-15.

Joseph in Prophetic Focus
Zechariah 12:10

Brave Joseph was like Jesus
In prophecies he made,
And just like Christ through envy
His kin upon him preyed.

Yes, truly he in type
Walked ways that Christ would tread:
By brethren was forsaken,
To Egypt sold, deemed dead.

There Satan wrought temptations
Through fleshly lusts men knew;
But he, like Christ, him parried,
In morals remained true.

Arrested as a rapist,
A liar then men heard,
Who banned him to a prison,
All patiently endured.

In prison there his wisdom
At length to pharaoh told,
He rose to world dominion
And kingly pow'r untold!

But still, like Christ uniquely,
He was to kin unknown
Until with their repentance
Forgiveness would be shown!

We'll see these types are proven
In time historically:
Christ Jesus too in favor,
Shall reign most gloriously!

The Saga of Israel, Thrice-born Now To Be
Eph. 2:1; 1 Cor. 15:1; Ezek 37:1-14; Rom. 11:15

On May fourteen in 'Forty-eight
The Jewish state was born.
Or can we now more truly state,
She was by God REBORN?

Yes, history in fact will tell
Three thousand years ago
The mighty people Israel
God's pow'r with men first showed.

But then an awful thing of dread—
Fate played her timeless tune—
Blest Isr'el, sinning, dropped down dead,
By dire declensions doomed!

Yet, friends, is this not true of ALL,
Of Adam's HUMAN RACE -
We're victims of a tragic fall
So look to God for grace?

And God, it's true, His grace has given,
So real to TWICE-BORN MEN,
As we like all from dread death riven
Now truly LIVE AGAIN!

YET ISR'EL BY THE WORD OF GOD
TWICE-BORN TOO FROM DEAD BONES
WILL ONE DAY KNOW HER LORD TO LAUD,
THRICE-BORN WITH JESUS OWNED!

My Hope for Israel's Future
Genesis 12:1-3; Zechariah 2:7, 8; Psalm 2:12; Romans 11:15, 26

Foes are seen so intense for the Jew's violence
That a redness must glow from their hands!
And they harbor such hate—such that cannot abate—
That they vow to "wipe them from the land!"
But I say, don't they know against God they do go
In the madness of mind for such war?
That He surely will choose to fully aid Jews
As the nation He's aided before?
Oh, thank God for their lot, that Messiah has bought
These His offspring with His Precious Blood!
That one day with their kiss they shall know kingdom bliss
As sweet nectar that flows from above!
But you ask me just why I with joy can rely
On a premise that such comes about?
Well, I know it's God's Word,
So from God I have heard—
And, my friend, that excludes any doubt!

Some Ask, "Is This to Be...."
"...No more sea...."—Rev. 21:1b; "I have placed my rainbow in the clouds...."—Gen. 9:13

Some ask, "Is this to be,
The hist'ry we shall see
Of sun, and wind, and water,
Destruction's mix for slaughter
Of men, our sons and daughters,
In hell of storm and sea?"

Oh no, let's look again
At God's Best Book for men:
We see the sea no more,
Nor Noah's flood of yore,
God's promise shuts that door -
His rainbow, our Amen!

The Message TO US IN KATRINA
Proverbs 14:34; Revelation 5, then thru 19

O Lord, You once had walked the waves
Of Galilee we know,
And howling winds and waves behaved
When you said, "Be it so!"

But, Oh our God, we are awe-struck
By cries now borne on air;
We now see oceans run amok,
Destruction everywhere!

But, Lord, since ancient times we say
That You are Lord of All,
Yet when to You Your people pray
These storms are seldom stalled!

Yes, saved souls pray, observing fasts—
Agreement too is found—
But storms don't stop, it seems alas!
And yet Your pow'r abounds!

Why cannot we then have more hope?
Our nation's in despair!
Your saints are clinging—NOT TO ROPES—
Please, Lord, WE KNOW YOU CARE?

"I, JESUS CHRIST, HAVE BEEN YOUR STAY,
HAVE BORNE FOR YOU SIN'S PAIN;
AND THOUGH I'D NOW PUT SUCH AWAY,
THE CURSE ON EARTH REMAINS!

"AND PRIDEFUL MAN AS YET UNBENDING,
STILL CLINGS SO TO HIS SIN;
SUCH CALLS FOR PLAGUES ON EARTH UNENDING,
INCLUDING WAVES AND WIND!

"BUT I'LL ONE DAY UNROLL GOD'S SCROLL
TO BUY BACK ALL SIN LOST,
AND THEN NO MORE YOU'LL SEE DEATH'S TOLL,
BUT TRIUMPHS THROUGH MY CROSS!"

When The Towers Fell

When The Towers fell what celebrations!
When The Towers fell what revelry!
When The Towers fell note demonstrations!
See the cultists clap with cruel glee!

When The Towers fell God marked elation,
And His prophets voiced dire, prophecy!
Hear these pledges of divine vexation—
Retribution on iniquity!

God's redeemed have blessed compensations;
Yes, they have a God-giv'n faith to see
JESUS CHRIST THE KING IN ADORATION -
AND COMING SOON IN TOTAL VICTORY!

Till "Come, Fly Away, My Love!"
Gen. 3:14a, 15b NW; Rev. 6:10b; I Thess 4:16a, 17a

Dear Lord, we're all so weary here
Of serpent pow'r and peril!
We want to hear the Victor's cheer,
And see Your flag unfurled!

Too long the martyr's cry is heard!
Too long the widow's wail!
Oh, Lord, we long to hear Your word
That Satan's way has failed!

His way must give way to Your pow'r
Who bruised Your Heel blood red.
Yes, he must have his final hour
When crushed shall be his head!

Then truly love shall have love's way;
Then lifted shall be the least;
Then justice here shall have its day
For bludgeoned man and beast!

But till that day, Our loving Lord,
Our focus is above
From which we'll hear that longed-for word:
"Come, fly away, my love!"

Arise, O Israel, and Quit Your Quaking!

Arise, O Israel, and quit your quaking
For millennial miseries!
For says Jehovah God, "You're not forsaken—
It's your year of Jubilee!"

(Chorus)
O hallelujah! O hallelujah!
Hallelujah, praise the Lord!
O hallelujah! O hallelujah!
Hallelujah, praise the Lord!

Yea, from the lion's mouth of your affliction
You are rescued and behold—
For sincerity of sin's contrition
Our God crowns you now with gold!

Chorus (above)

Praise God, you'll eat the feast withheld by Satan
As your age-long enemy!
And you shall drink the drink of pure elation—
O'er him total victory!

Chorus (above)

Rejoice, for Christ the King and your Redeemer
Greets you with full liberty!
And you shall reign with Him long to remember—
O a thousand years to be!

Chorus (repeat twice)

Pray for Jerusalem's Peace
"Pray for the peace of Jerusalem; they shall prosper that love thee."—
Psa. 122:6

"The more we get together
The happier we shall be,"
Is true, and ill will betters
When Bible based, I see.
But if based on concession
To lies that we have heard,
From Scripture learn God's lesson,
Reality's sure word:

The worst lie in all plainness
In minds of mortal men
Brands Israel for arraignment
For malice once again;
That with apartheid policies
Of ill will toward her foes
She only is a devotee
To selfish ends of old.

But, no, she has, as facts are known,
Extended her right hand,
Promoting peace toward neighbors, shown
By giving up her lands.
From ancient times this too we'd note:
To curse her, as God's friend,
Can only mean ourselves we smote
With curses in the end!

But, Lord, we pray please help Your seed,
Brave Israel, in world courts,
That we shall see a basic need
Of honest world support.
That too we'll never ever find
Agreement with her foes,
But, rather, with God's word to mind
We'll plead, "Lord, end her woes!"

Christ's Second Coming
"When you see all these things, know He is near even at the door."
Luke 13:3

Tsunamis, floods, and hurricanes,
Huge wildfires in the news,
Dire plagues and hunger, wars to blame,
Cause fear and minds confuse.
Then add men's moral bankruptcy—
High churchmen not immune!—
False cults, their christs and heresies,
Are these sure signs of doom?

A single sign men might ignore
But all collectively
Must tell us Christ is "at the door,"
His coming soon to be.

At Length "The Paint Must Dry!"
Isa. 11:6-9; Hab. 2:14 NKJV

A doughty dame of days bygone
Still states (as others sigh)
That though the right by most's made wrong,
"At length the paint must dry!"

I'm sure this means with passing time
God's good will comes to term,
And then at length God's paradigm
Of right will then be learned.

And, oh I pray, God haste the day,
As Your Word prophesies,
That righteousness when in full sway
Shall this world sanctify!

CHAPTER FIVE: "A LITTLE HUMOR NOW AND THEN...."

Someone of note in the past has said "A little humor now and then is relished by the best of men," and, friends, I think that anonymous person was certainly right. God in fact it was Who placed within man the ability to laugh, a gift not given animals (except "the laughing hyena"?—not really!); and in His Word it is also said that "a merry heart does good like medicine." Yes, believe me, I have heard of someone in the past, their death having been declared to be imminent due to some disease, who decided to try laughing himself to health. And I understand he succeeded! Well, I'm sure this won't always be the good result of laughing, but, nonetheless, I do contend that laughter has a real benefit for those who in their difficulties will let a bit more of it into their lives.

As I've quoted some humorist of the past many times, I reiterate the quote now: "God must have had a sense of humor, since otherwise He wouldn't have created the monkeys, myrrh cats, parrots, otters, skunks and — not to mention yours truly — **SOME OF YOU FOLKS OUT THERE IN MY AUDIENCE!**"

With that in mind, friends, I feel that some good clean stories, incidents, plays on words, etc.—poems that might be classified as "jokes"—can do some good in my volume of poems; and therefore I include the following section dedicated to these. I hope they enhance your appreciation of my anthology as a whole...and so they follow.

So just you wipe that frown off your face and give your face "a lift," hear? I think you'll be pleased with the result!

Thanks for God's Good Humor

Does our God ever laugh with good humor?
Does He chuckle and chortle with glee?
Well, Who was it Who made skunks and monkeys?
And, moreover, Who made you and me?

I say, surely God has His good humor—
Beyond that though, His love is most real;
After all, didn't Jesus leave Heaven
For that cross with our sadness to heal?

And that cross, it was no laughing matter!
Hear our Lord as He cries from that tree:
"O My God! Why am I here so forsaken?"
As He died there for our misery!

As God laughs, we can laugh; it's a tonic.
And thank God it helps some in our need—
But for healing from sin look to Jesus,
Who died for Men's fatal disease!

On Second Thought....!

O they say all that God has created is good,
For they seem to work well, understood.
But I think that that "all" could look better as "most,"
For some things just seem bad—well, at least they come close!
Yes, take lice, poison ivy, cock roaches, most bugs;
And of course yucky things like those most sluggish slugs;
Take mosquitoes, house flies, stinging ants, pesky gnats;
Take those moles, slinking snakes, and of course filthy rats!

But, on second thought....Here now repenting I moan—
THROUGH THOSE PESTS HERE
I LONG FOR GOD'S HEAVEN AND HOME!

Some Poetic Church Bloopers

Our church choir will be singing,
"Our God Still Helps Us Yet."
Join the choir and you'll help their singing—.
They need all they can get!

For this sale, ladies, bring
The discards from your house.
Of course also bring
Each one her own spouse!

Our Miss Jones sang her song,
"Ill Soon Be Leaving Here,"
After which it was seen
The whole church rose to cheer.

A pot luck dinner we've planned
For our big celebration,
After which Pastor Jones
Will give some medications.

This noon you'll hear a sermon,
"There's Hope in All Life's Crunch,"
But first join us at mealtime, friends—
We're heaving one great lunch!

Our church choir will be singing,
"What Life's all About."
Let's give each member praises
When we later pass out.

How About These "Burma Shave Signs"?

My name's not Taylor—
I won't evade
But Heaven for me
Is tailor made!

Christian, always
"Keep the faith!"
Except with sinners—
To them relate!

If cookin' is
Your callin', Ma'am,
Forbidden fruit
Makes one bad jam!

When it's so late
And you can't sleep,
Then count your blessings—
Not those dumb sheep!

God's "Thou Shalt Nots"
Are for your good.
What part of "not"
Ain't understood?

If truth decay
Finds you so li'ble,
Then, hey "brush up"
There on your Bible!

Wal-Mart saves money
We are told,
But try my Christ—
He'll SAVE YOUR SOUL!

You say you're shook
In life's mad race?
Hey, Moses was
A basket case!

Jesus lovers
Tithe, I'd say.
"Honk for Christ"?—
The shirkers way!

It's his first time
To go to church;
Too bad he's goin'
In a hearse!

The vitamin
For saints, my son,
Is simply said,
Just you B-1!

If Hell you'd miss
And heat concernin',
Exposure to
The Son stops burnin'!

Ode on the Existence of Lice from Earliest Times Till Now

Adam
Had 'em;
Eve
Grieved!
(The above could probably go into the <u>Guinness Book of Records</u>
as the shortest poem on record—with the longest title!—JE)

Pets and "That Bad Hair Day"

I'll go to bat for my pet cats—
(Yes, dogs too would belong!),
They never have "that bad hair day"
When they must sing sad songs!

Oh no, unlike us human folk,
Who often come off grumpy,
Our pets don't pout, have doleful doubts—
They're always cheerful, chummy!

If just the night before you had
To put them out the door;
With morning light your face in sight,
They love you all the more!

No, they don't for us grudges keep—
In fact THEY DON'T HAVE ANY!
They take us whether good or bad,
With wealth or sans a penny!

"O if I had my druthers, friends,
I tell you what I'd do:
I'd take my pets to Heav'n to share
God's best with me and you!"

A Saturday Morning's Muttering

A "friend" of mine while acting generously
Had bought for me a very special gift.
This morning—Saturday!—quite vigorously
The thing "began to crow" right on my wrist!

Why no, my friends, "this rooster" isn't red,
But hey like one its "crowing's" most abrupt!
Ten times, I think, it "crowed" there by my head
Unseemly like, insisting I get up!

Now sulking with my coffee I need cheer;
I'm muttering, "Oh my, I'm such a wreck!
If this my watch indeed were Chanticleer,
I think that I with joy would wring its neck!"

It's oft in life we think some gifts are great;
And some like mine we'd classify as worse.
A bible fact, "In morning we all hate
The early yells of wakers—they're a curse!"

"He that blesseth his friend with a loud voice, rising early in the morning, it shall be counted as a curse to him."—Proverbs 27:14!

Watch Out for Those Fruit Peels!
"The foxes, the little foxes...spoil the vines."—Solomon's Song 2:15
"...Who has despised the day of small things?"—Zech. 4:10

There once was a stuntman named Leach
Whose life leaves a lesson to teach.
He survived some great perils—
Over Niagara in a barrel!—
But succumbed from a slip on the street!

Oh, dear friends, this one lesson I'd say,
We should gain as our lesson today:
Though great tests find our nerves so well steeled,
We must be careful of little fruit peels,
AND SMALL SINS THAT CAN KILL 'LONG LIFE'S WAY!

Confession of a "Cracked Pot"
Jeremiah 18:3-6 ; 2 Corinthians 5:17

The Great Potter has said we're as "clay" on His wheel
And in need of new molding our souls thus to heal,
For you see we've been marred by the first Adam's fall,
So a brand new creation is needed by all!

To the Potter the wheel is life's total events
In the which He would form us to His blest intents.
If by Him not refashioned—oh, no one's excepted!—
It's Gehenna's sad end where we're "potsherds," rejected!

Well, my friends, God is calling to you now today;
Through His word He is asking that you humbly pray:
"Oh, Great Potter, this sinner's gone wrong, I now see.
Oh, remake me, forgive me—a new man I would be!

"I most humbly do ask this in Jesus' blest Name,
Who once died for my sins my soul thus to reclaim!"
This poor poet so prayed and now has a watchword:
It's although I've been cracked, I'm not lost like potsherds!

I am God's new creation through Christ and His cross.
Gehenna is gone! I've new life—I'm not lost!
With my sad soul reshapen, great blessing I see—
Oh how great is the potter who refashioned me!

Jim Once Said

Jim once said, "I'm not well;
I KNOW I'm not fit!"
On his tombstone it reads:
"SEE, I SAID I WAS SICK!"

Some say, "John, you're a fool
To love Jesus so true!"
Well, whaddya say—
JUST WHOSE FOOL ARE YOU?

At Bat with "Saints Alive"

Our dear class, "Saints Alive,"
May lack vigor and jive
When at eighty at baseball we mingle,
But when we come to bat
It won't matter all that –
We will still get our hits, though they're singles!

After plodding to first
We don't stand and rehearse:
"Should we steal second base?" don't you see.
For the pain in our joints
Will for sure make the point
That our legs look at life honestly!

Heading home round third base,
After singles well placed,
We don't listen at yells of the locals.
Oh no, we will try
To make home base or die—
Trusting we can find it with bifocals!

But if we should strike out,
We don't sit down and pout,
For the rules say we still have the time
To come up anew
Making singles we're due,
For the innings they still number nine!

So we urge you, our friends,
Who like us use Depends—
Don't you give up with nerves all atingle!
When that dude throws the ball,
Don't you swing for the wall,
We know home runs don't win—get a single!

God's Gift in MARMALADE

The gifts that God the Giver gives
Are always "tailor made,"
And so mine is affirmative—
For me it's MARMALADE!

A cat, he's cast in orange and brown
(As by his name portrayed).
With poet's pen I here propound
God's gift is MARMALADE!

I say, "Yeah, he's 'the cat's meow!'
Except to serenade,
So silent did he come somehow,
My muted MARMALADE!"

Yes, he came here without a voice!
But, no, I'm not dismayed,
For how he purrs!—and I rejoice
In motored MARMALADE!

Also he's failed to climb one tree—
So squirrels fear no raid!—
Resulting he's well-rounded, see
My fulsome MARMALADE!

But yet when to my lap he leaps
This cat I can't upbraid.
We share the peace when there he sleeps,
This restful MARMALADE!

And always when put out at night
A loyalty's displayed—
For comes the dawn with its first light
There's faithful MARMALADE!

Praise God, my cat—here scorning rats!—
Some SERPENTS has displayed;
Yes, snakes he brings to my doormat—
Spiritual MARMALADE!

O would that all of this world were
Like my cat Spirit made;
This world for sure would be secure
If more like MARMALADE!

The Holiday for Atheists

A certain man, an atheist,
In spirit most unawed
Had brought a suit against theists
Who have great perks in God.

For instance, this man saw we had
Our holidays each year,
While atheists indeed felt bad
Because they'd none to cheer.

He didn't like Thanksgiving Day,
Nor days with Jewish joys.
He'd clap if Easter went away,
Yule too for girls and boys.

This suitor's judge there on the bench
(This case he did deplore!).
Saw this sad suitor, quest unquenched,
Pursue him out the door.

"You want a day to soothe your thirst?"
This judge asked him so cool.
"Well, how about our April first?—
It's there for April fools!"

"The Bible, which you overrule,
And Lord, Whom you won't laud,
Indeed both say that you are fools
Who say 'There is no God!'"

God's Recall of Humans Here Read

As Creator of humans God issues recall
Of each unit due to awesome need.
With a most fatal flaw in the heart shown by all,
He alerts that all give earnest heed.
Many symptoms discovered are herewith made known,
And each human is urged to assess:
"Is there any here shown as with others who moan?"
May God help us to all take His test:

"There is lack of attention to foul voice emissions,
A forgetting of one's origin.
There is lack of direction for duty or mission,
Racial hatred discovered 'mongst them;
All too often there's blame and so little of shame
For those lustful acts thoughtlessly done;
Depression suppressed is deep set in the breast,
With base fear and gross boasting oft known;
There is love for the less—none for God Who is best
Which are idols, My manual has shown!

"Now just one certain flaw can mean that unit's lost,
Though in others one thinks he is clear;
Oh, your Lord cautions care lest one counts not the cost
That such thinking has grounds for great fear.
But in lieu of this dictum fact-finders find fault
That all men, SAVE ONE MAN, have sure need;
And that One, Great physician, came on Calv'ry's mission
That we all for heart healing may plead!"

Oh, dear friends, if we here would ignore God's recall,
End results are too awful to tell—
Except ruin for wrecks must await there for all
In that junkyard our Lord labeled Hell.

"For whoever shall keep the whole law, and yet stumble in one point, he is guilty of all."—James 2:10 NKJV; "And in hell he lifted up his eyes, being in torments...."—Luke 16:23.

Some Could-Be and Would-Be Epitaphs

Here sleeps a good friend,
Dentist Bill O'Cassidy.
Till released there in Heaven
BILL HERE FILLS HIS LAST CAVITY!

Walt Williams here fought
Forest fires with great care.
He had hopes he'd not fight
THE SAME FLAMES OVER THERE!

This good baker once kneaded
A lot of good bread,
But here found HE MOST NEEDED
CHRIST GOD'S LIVING BREAD!

Clem sought homes for his clients;
To such was addicted.
He's trusting IN HEAVEN
HE'LL NOT BE EVICTED!

Joe played basketball here
With vigor and vim—
But not against Jesus—
HE'D TEAMED UP WITH HIM!

Bertilucci on earth
Could repair any sole,
But down here he made sure
HIS OWN SOUL WAS MADE WHOLE!

Yes, Isaac could fly,
As all true pilots can;
BUT HE KNOWS "THE SKY PILOT"
AND HIS FUTURE FLIGHT PLAN!

A tax gatherer here,
Rick found little relaxing,
But he knows that in Heaven
IT WON'T BE ALL THAT TAXING!

For that "Gift of Criticism"

The faithful preacher preached upon
The subject of "God's Gifts"
And hoped thereby the usefulness
Of his small flock to lift.

"Beloved of God," he did exhort,
"At least one gift each of us owns,
And one or more we must use for
Our Lord upon His throne!"

Then later at the door he heard,
"My one gift's criticism."
To which the pastor proffered then
A bit of Bible wisdom:

"Friend, do you know the parable
Our Lord gave of the pounds?
Of one who had a single gift
But hid it in the ground?"

"Of course I know the Bible, sir;
But what do you advise?"
"My son, I'd say with this YOUR 'GIFT,'
Please go and do likewise."

Let's Be Positive, My Friends!

If room you'd give to gloominess,
There's gloom to make one glum!
If glow you would in righteousness,
By joy you'll overcome!

The devil finds his great delight
In negativities!
The Lord of Hosts displays His might
With positives, I see!

A little lesson comes to mind
Whereby this truth unfolds:
To doughnuts fine most are inclined,
WHILE SOME JUST SEE THE HOLES!

CHAPTER SIX: POEMS DEDICATED IN MEMORY OF CHERISHED FAMILY AND FRIENDS

Joyce, my wife, has stuck by me and for me for more than fifty-eight years now, and I especially want to include a few poems dedicated to her whom I have loved and do indeed now love the more! She has certainly been a tower of strength to me in difficult times in our lives together, and this I would not ignore, could not ignore in this book of poems.

Also my dear mother of yesteryear, a once long-lost friend from my Marine Corps days, a grandson, and others generally who have loved me and been cherished by me, I now want to give remembrance to here in this anthology. I hope all reading this section of my book will enjoy poems dedicated to these.

Along that line someone has asked, "Will we know one another in Heaven?" and my answer is, "Yes!". Paul in I Thessalonians 4 says we shall be caught up "together to meet the Lord in the air," and I think this suggests what I believe addresses the matter. Also, in the Old Testament, again and again believers are said to be "gathered to their fathers" at death; now, doesn't this say something positively on the question, friends? Well, I think so.

Yes, we shall renew old friendships and loves of the past in Heaven, friends and loved ones long since gone from our lives perhaps. Up there we will know one another as we're known now by our Heavenly Father, recalling our good times, laughing at trials then seen as nothing, etc., etc., as together we especially worship Christ, our eternally most cherished Lover and Friend!

Life Has Told We Are Old, Yellowed, Sere, Darling

Life has told we are old, yellowed, sere, darling:
Autumn leaves frayed by frost, soon to fall.
But to me you're as gold, mellowed here, darling:
Beauteous fruit, golden good, best of all!

When our God's hallowed hand shall reach down, darling,
Winter woes thus to go in His care,
Should I be waiting here or up there, darling,
Soon we'll be joined again Heav'n to share!

If I Could Seize a Sunbeam

If I could seize a sunbeam
To help you, dear, today,
I'd grasp one for your trials
And brighten up your way.

If I could form a river
Set it flowing for your aid,
I'd bring such to your door, dear,
To bless the plans you've laid.

If I were God's strong angel,
I'd heed your faintest call,
Toss cares into the ocean
And rid you of them all.

But, dear, I'm not an angel,
Can't aid as said above,
But I can give a hug, dear,
While offering my love.

And I can ask our Father,
Who knows your ev'ry care,
To help you from His Heaven—
I pledge to you my prayer.

"Joyce, M.R.S.!"

I recall a GREAT MAN known as ONE in the past
Though not lettered of men, but with talents so vast;
Here his gifts I ascribe to my darling wife, Joyce,
She unlettered also but in God surely "Choice!"
True four offspring plus husband she helped "get through school,"
As she "stayed by the stuff," pledging her aid to pool.
Then, all totaled, her five gained for selves ten degrees,
While she, faithful at home, showed that she was well pleased.
So now here in our old age I'll say I've been blest
To have loved **whom I letter as "JOYCE, M.R.S.!"**

A Question Resolved

I recall of my mother in days long of yore
Once dividing an apple in quarters to eat,
And then giving them all to four children adored,
While I wondered why she disliked apples so sweet.

Well, it's now looking back that the fact become clear
That it wasn't that apples to taste were so poor—
Yes, the thought brings her back and makes her the more dear—
I know now that my mom loved her children much more!

"Grandpa, What Do We Know About Heaven....?

"Grandpa, what do we know about Heaven to be?"
My young grandson named Evan asked me.
"Will we wear jeans up there? Have shaved heads or long hair?
What will friends, when they look at us see?

"Must we go there to school with our homework not done?
Do we sleep all the time with no fun?
Are our skateboards allowed? Do we just sit on clouds?
Can we play ball and hit a homerun?"

You can say I was challenged as tackling my task!
Uhhh, I pondered the questions he'd asked.
I had studied God's Book, of its wisdom partook,
And recalled from the wealth of that cache....

"Well, our clothes, I would deem, will be best ever seen,
With our hair I'd say great, just supreme!
In our looks none could trace a lone zit on our face—
We'll look better than Hollywood's seen!

"As for schoolwork up there—not allowed it's been shown;
Gone are book bags with their tiring tomes!
Mute are preachers who preach and teachers who teach,
For 'We'll know then as now we are known!'

"No, we'll not sit on clouds—boredom's there not allowed!—
We'll serve Jesus with gifts He's endowed.
We'll give Him all the praise throughout all Heaven's days,
Of Him boast while of self never proud!

"As for fun, there'll be joy, as the Bible reports—
Spirit-joy which is better than sports'!
We will know we've sure won when we hear Christ's 'Well done!'
We'll shout 'Vict'ry!' with grandstand supports!

"But one final fact, Evan, if Heaven you'd win
You must have as your Savior from sin
Christ Who for YOU once died, all your sins thus to hide,
If not, Evan, you'll never get in!"

Well, I'm glad I can say Evan's saved since he prayed,
Took on Christ as our Heaven's 'One Way!'
Yes, he's made the right choice, indeed now can rejoice
With the first-fruits of Heaven today!

Friends Are Friends Forever

I was abashed when out the past
A friend came by today.
Some fifty years—yes, with some tears—

Had come and gone, I'd say,
Since we had dined in auld lang syne,
In sanguine yesterday.

We both have thrived with Christian wives,
And have sure hope to see
Joys without end with life's Best Friend
We'd both claimed mutually.
Oh my it's good this brotherhood
With loved ones e'er to be!

My Joyce

Some many years ago in Dayton, Ohio,
A marriage was made in June,
When God in His love gave to me from above
My bride, His choicest boon.

Well, she's been with me long, sanctified many a wrong,
Blessed me with heart, hand, and voice;
And children they came each bearing my name—
I love her, this woman, my Joyce!

Now our children are grown, have young of their own—
Grandchildren—in these we rejoice.
She's blessed them all too; her touch they all knew—
I love her, this woman, my Joyce!

Life's day now grows short. Soon comes time to report
To my God— what words for my choice?
To Him I shall say, "Thank you, Father, always—
I love her, this woman, my Joyce!"

"Hold Onto Your Fork!"

Our Mom she was the gourmet's one tremendous cook.
For getting up a dinner, she was "the best in the book!"
The salad, soup, and veggies she'd serve, and maybe some pork—
And then she would say,
"Dessert's on the way!
Pass those dirty dishes—
But do hold onto your fork!"

At our Thanksgiving dinners, I tell you we'd sure get our fill!
The turkey was surely sumpt'ous, with many a gastric thrill!
But before our Dad got started on "autos, wrenches, and torque,"
You'd hear our Mom say,
"Dessert's on the way!
Pass those dirty dishes—
But do hold onto your fork!"

Christmas at our house was special, with all things your heart to please:
Delights for the eyes, and for the ears, and presents under the tree.
At dinner we all were so happy—without ever "poppin' a cork!"
Then our Mom would say,
"Dessert's on the way!
Pass those dirty dishes—
But do hold onto your fork!"

Through our young years it was always the same—happy at our house!
Then Mom got sick and passed away, and, truly, our spirits were doused!
We all were so very unhappy—till the fun'ral with Pastor O'Rourke,
When we heard him say,
"Dessert's Mom's today;
She's 'passed her dirty dishes,'
AND IN HEAVEN SHE'S USING 'HER FORK!'"

Now I cannot know what drives you, your personal aspirations;
Are you wishing for wealth, or social rank, maybe some great citation?
Or perhaps it could be for fam'ly, "a visit from the stork?"
Be that as it may,
Dessert's coming my way;
The Lord's taken my dirty dishes—
FOR MOM'S HEAVEN I'M HOLDIN' MY FORK!

Together Again

Should you go ahead,
And I stay instead
To mourn you,
Walk slowly, my dear,
While I follow here
In the path.
And listen for me
To so eagerly
Call your name.
Then when you turn around
I'll make up the ground
To join you.
Arm in arm then we'll go
Into Heaven to know
Our God's welcome.
There together we'll sing;
Forever we'll bring
Our God all the praise!

But should I lead the way
Toward that halcyon day
We call Heaven,
I'll walk slowly for you
As I asked you to do
Once for me.
And I'll listen with care
For your call as a prayer
From behind me.
Turned, what joy to behold
That girl who of old
Shared all my dreams!
Arm in arm then we'll go
Into Heaven to know
Our God's welcome.
There together we'll sing;
Forever we'll bring
Our God all the praise!

CHAPTER SEVEN: "GOD'S BEST IS YET TO BE"—WE'VE HEAVEN TO COME!

Psalm 103 presents a litany of blessings that we have in our God and Savior Jesus Christ, and it is wonderful! There we read of forgiveness of sins, healing oftentimes in answer to prayer, protection in danger by His angels (a reality according to Hebrews 1), His loving kindness encouraging us day by day, mercy instead of wrath for sins committed too often each day, good food for our appetites, His word to guide us, etc. etc. – and to think that we still with all that's said and done HAVE HEAVEN TO COME TO CROWN IT ALL!

O yes, friends, I know we have trials too, sicknesses often, persecution sometimes for our faithfulness to Christ, but I think of the words of a song we've all probably heard:

"It will be worth it all When we see Jesus; each trial will
seem so small when we see Christ. One look at His dear face
each sorrow will erase. So bravely run the race till we see
Christ!"

Yes, that's what our next-to-last grouping of poems in our anthology is all about. We have Heaven to come of which we read that "Eye has not seen, nor ear heard, nor have entered into the heart of man the things God has prepared for those who love Him."—1 Corinthians 2:9. I hope in this section of my poems I "touch the hem of the garment" of those blessings yet to come in Heaven which God's saints one day for sure will all know. O yes, there is no doubt that 100% of those who have been redeemed shall enter one day "into the joy of our Lord!" Read the so-inadequate representation of this herein and praise God with me!

"God's Best Is Yet to Be!"

I here recall from out my past
Some words of poetry;
In all life's tasks in these I've basked:
"God's best is yet to be!"

But then as down life's way I've come
I've seen some shadowy sod;
Here near overcome by things leaving me numb,
I've been saved by my faith in God!

In business dealings of yesteryear—
Omitting earnest prayers—
I've suffered here so much in cheer
For lack of good caution and care.

In bodily ills I've had some bad calls
(Ole "Arthur," of course, in attack).
I've seen three bad falls, and clinching it all
Malaria once set me back!

But now at eighty three I've had aid,
Except for my two "gimpy legs!"
My doc, dismayed, for me has assayed,
"For real problems I'll give you 'goose eggs!'"

But still I know what lies ahead
As far as all life is concerned:
There'll be bad bugs in my flower beds
Until my "last shovel is turned!"

So until that day this one thing I'll say
With my God I'll go on this to see:
His grace I'll know as onward I go—
And "God's best is yet to be!"

When Born Men Here Are Seen to Be

When born men here are seen to be
The people of broad destinies.
We first live lives on earth, and then
A second life for ALL begins.
The Christian's life "up there" seen hence
Is "so much better" from common sense.
Yes, Heav'n for saved folks serves them well—
But for the lost!—a horror, ____!

Of present lives we have in mind,
The Christian's too excels, we find:
When "born again," a peace profound
Abundantly in Christ is found;
In Him we win o'er nicotine,
Yes, other drugs, and drink's extremes;
And then, too, gambling must give way
Where many find earth's "hell to pay";

Potentially we have the best
Of fam'ly life, the marriage nest;
We oft live long while praising God,
Good mem'ries known—in some so flawed!

The better lives are ours, you see—
But not so automatic'ly:
With FAITH IN CHRIST all flags unfurl:
WE LIVE THE BEST OF SEV'RAL WORLDS!

When "The Shadows Flee Away"

"Until the day breaks, and the shadows flee away, return hastily my beloved... like a roe or a young hart over the mountains.... "—Canticles 2:17 TAB

Though enemies my way surrounds
With damning curses all around,
I'll still believe Christ's love abounds
Till "The shadows flee away!"

Yes, friends may fail me, neighbors too;
Loved ones may leave while blame ensues—
But there's His love to help renew
Till "The shadows flee away!"

Bad suits and settlements may stun,
And woes may see my way undone,
But faith remains till Heav'n I've won
Till "The shadows flee away!"

Grave sickness likewise may cause loss,
While accidents my ways may cross,
But I'll view all of this but dross
Till "The shadows flee away!"

Then I shall worship with great praise,
And serve My Love through endless days—
And oh the songs my heart shall raise
When "The shadows flee away!"

How Big We'll Win When We Shall Die!

They say, "This life's a losing game -
Great losses known that once were claimed!"
And true we'll lose our health,
And then at last our wealth—
But what a lot we'll gain in Jesus' Name!

As seniors we'll lose muscles' might,
Together with our appetites.
Though true we'll lose good looks
(As told in God's Good Book)—
How well we'll look in Heaven's light!

So, friends, let's hold Christ's banner high
And squelch those faithless sobs and sighs.
Some day up there we'll shout—
With things already turned about!
HOW BIG WE'LL WIN WHEN WE SHALL DIE!

Like Noah's Dove I've Found No Ease
"The dove found no resting place on which to roost, and she returned unto him , Noah, in the ark."—Genesis 8:9 TAB

Like Noah's dove I've found no ease,
As in fruitless flight I've flown
O'er many a mile of restless sea,
In search of my heart's home.

Man's wreck and ruin's everywhere,
Results of dire sin's costs,
And no one's here to breathe a prayer
For mercy midst this loss!

Dear Lord, alone in Thee is found
Sweet rest my wings to lend!
My feet would gain faith's solid ground—
O Lord, please take me in!

The Burial of Little Rosa Rodriguez
"A little child shall lead them."—Isaiah 11:6

Slowly to the burial site
Walked the heartbroken father,
Amidst the gloom of death's dark night,
To bury his six-year-old daughter.

His sweet little Rosa was dead;
Perished was his "Little Flower,"
Upon whose attentions his heart had fed,
Bringing joy to each day's long hard hours!

Yes, believe it, she was gone,
Unsmiling and cold in that coffin!
But how could his house still to him be home?
How could such a blow ever soften?

Arriving at the mocking plot
And the gaping hole which beckoned,
Came just a few with this man distraught,
Where mortality's dues would be reckoned!

Placed in his hand was a little key
To his little one's final enclosure,
Which, using, he viewed, then kissed the cold cheek,
Sobbing, "Good-bye, Little Flower, forever!"

The graveside service was done,
And the pastor spoke to the father:
"Kind sir, may I, just one on one,
Console you now for your daughter?

"Little Rosa's spirit has gone above
To bloom in God's garden in Heaven,
Where all little children have His special love,
So her spirit to God you have given.

"But one day King Jesus will cleave
The clouds with His key to ev'ryone's casket,
And a new, deathless body your girl will receive—
And He'll heal your hurts, too, if you'll ask it.

"He came long ago and died one day,
There bearing on His cross all our shame;
But He rose from death to take sins away
As we call upon His name.

"To us now—adults—He also can show
The same love He bestows on our children;
And I'm praying that you—and others—may know
The truth that 'A small child shall lead them.'

"You see, Little Rosa is now with her God,
But she'd like you to join her in Heaven.
And there you will be—on Heaven's same sod—
If you've faith in Christ's sacrifice given."

Praise God, once again, as quite often the case,
A small child with her faith indeed led him;
And there's dancing where children behold their God's face—
AND I'VE A FEELING OUR ROSA THERE LEADS THEM!

Enraptured at Death
"O death, where is thy sting? O grave, where is thy victory?"
—1 Cor. 2:9

Is this that "death" which I so feared to see?
That which I'd hoped sweet rapture would forestall?
'Tis true, though seen as Jesus said 'twould be:
"Our vict'ry—shared together!"—at His call!

Unknown delights not sensed where eagles soar
Are mine so freely now in fluid flight!
I see the sights unsung in earthly lore,
All pain now past of mortals' tear-filled nights!

I thrill where body ills can harm no more,
Where hurtful words can nevermore benumb!
I raise my praise to Him Whom I adore,
While strumming strings the blest can only strum!

ENRAPTURED THAT WITH CHRIST I'VE TASTED DEATH,
I JOY WITH JESUS, BREATHING HEAVEN'S BREATH!

When "Down Time's" Mine at Last

When I think how this wrangler's life's nigh spent,
With year of "three score ten"* I can relate;
When buckaroos have long since pitched THEIR tents
But time's still MINE—right now I calculate—
I wonder what for me would be the best?
While heart's still tickin', what should be my aim?
Should I give place to dude-ranch rowdiness,
Here spending much on self while strength remains?
Oh no, The Trail Boss there demands accountin'
Of gifts, allotments, time, and talents spent!

When to the pay-off point Ole Paint I'm mountin'
I'd not be off with woeful sad lament!
Instead, God, help that I'll be here still hustlin',
Still roundin' up "the stragglers" per Your task,
That at Trails End I'll have good conscience trustin'
To hear "Well done!" when "down time's"** mine at last!

*"The days of our years are three-score years and ten."—Psa. 90:10;
**There remains...rest for the people of God."—Heb. 4:9.

My Epitaph
"His servants shall serve Him."--Rev. 22:3

My house is quite small now,
With no spare room at all now,
And kind people step over my wee roof of sod.
But don't think that I'm sad now--
No, I'm supremely glad now!
For through Jesus my spirit is Home now with God!

My Home is so grand here!
With all good things at hand here!
God's angel-choir helping my Savior to laud!
I don't have any fear here--
And how could I shed tear here?!--
While serving my Savior at Home here with God!

CHAPTER EIGHT:
SOME ORIGINAL SONGS GOD HAS GIVEN ME

I suppose the biggest surprise of my retirement years as an inexperienced and untrained musician was a period of a few years when in my seventies God gave me some songs, original songs, that follow here in sheet music form in my efforts to glorify Him. Music has always meant much to me. Yes, I recall my dear mother's going about the house singing the good songs of Zion; and I'd say "the fruit didn't fall far from the tree" in my case. I love the old hymns of the church too. My wife and I go monthly to two nursing homes here in Jacksonville where she plays the piano and I lead out in the old songs that she and I love—and so many of our friends there, older like myself, love so much too. I hope you will open up a little part of your heart to my humble efforts that follow. These, for me at least, have "set my heart a dancing" often since God gave them to me some several years ago.

Christmas Means 'Welcome Home!'

Words and Music by
John W. Evans

1. When Mary and Joseph that day
   To Bethlehem's inn made their way,
   Their homeless needs there were spurned,
   So still they searched, tired and worn,
   Till at last in a stable the world's Great Savior was born!

2. If today finds you sin-sick, so poor,
   And the world's denied you rest at its door;
   Come to Christ; don't delay,
   He won't turn you away!
   In His Heart you'll find love's meaning, That day will be your Christmas day!

© Copyright 2000 by John W. Evans, 7907 Jamaica Rd., N.,
Jacksonville, FL 32216. All rights reserved.

Refrain

Now, Christmas means "Welcome Home!" to-day for me; "Welcome Home!" from wand'ring in sin's mis-er-y. My Lord came for my loss, For my sin's cru-el cross, That I might share in His des-ti-ny, And sing God's praise in Heav-en's Home e-ter-nal-ly. Oh, Christmas means "Welcome Home!" to-day for me!

Jesus Walked My Calvary Road

Words and Music by
John W. Evans

O my Lord came in love's sweet-est sto-ry, From great hon-or, where there is no sin; Yes, He walked streets of gold there in glo-ry, Then He stepped down to walk a-mong men. But that Cal-va-ry road, what a bit-ter, bit-ter road, Where my Je-sus was there so op-pressed! But He walked it a-lone. For my sins to a-tone, Now I'm freed from those sins, I am blessed!

© Copyright 2000 by John W. Evans, 7907 Jamaica Rd., N., Jacksonville, FL 32216. All rights reserved.

Jesus Walked My Calvary Road - 2

CHORUS

I am blessed! I am blessed! O thank God, I am blessed, For my Lord car-ried there my sin's load! Yes, He walked up that Hill, Where His Pre-cious blood was spilled, O thank God, Je-sus walked my Cal-v'ry road!

Once a-gain my Lord walks there in glo-ry, With great hon-or where there is no sin, But my heart turns a-gain to that sto-ry, How He stepped down to walk a-mong men. But, oh, that

155

F/C C C
Cal-va-ry road, what a bit-ter, bit-ter road, Where my Je-sus was there so op-
G G7 C F/C C C7 F B♭/F F Fm6
pressed! But He walked it a-lone For my sins to a-tone, Now I'm
C/G C/E F C/G G7 C
freed from those sins, I am blessed!
CHORUS
C F/C Fm6/C C C7
I am blessed! I am blessed! O thank
F C C C/E F Fm G7sus G7
God, I am blessed, For my Lord car-ried there my sin's load! When He
C F/C C G7 Am G7 C7 F Fm6
walked up that Hill, Where His Pre-cious blood was spilled, O thank
C/E E♭°7 Dm7 G7 C F Fm6 C/E E♭°7 Dm7 G7 C
God, Je-sus walked my Cal-v'ry road! I thank God, Je-sus walked my Cal-v'ry road!

He Chose My Cross, Not His Crown

Words and Music by
John W. Evans

1. Our dear Lord in the Bi-ble says, "For all things give thanks." So for all things I'm grate-ful, But as the high-est in rank Is the fact that in Heaven My name's writ-ten down, Be-cause Je-sus on Cal-v'ry Chose my cross, not His crown.

2. Now ev-'ry day is Thanks-giv-ing Since His love gripped my heart, And I'm e-quipped for liv-ing With a new-birth jump-start. Yes, for Heav'n I am bound, And sing Christ's praise on my way, He chose my cross, not His crown, There on Cal-v'ry that day.

© Copyright 2000 by John W. Evans, 7907 Jamaica Rd., N. Jacksonville, FL 32216. All rights reserved.

He Chose My Cross, Not His Crown - 2

REFRAIN

He chose my cross, not His crown, There on Cal-v'ry that day; He chose my cross, not His crown When He could have walked a-way! Now for heav'n I am bound, And sing Christ's praise on my way. He chose my cross, not His crown, There on Cal-v'ry that day.

That Old Romans Road

Romans 3:23; 6:23; 5:8; 10:9, 10

Words and Music by
John W. Evans

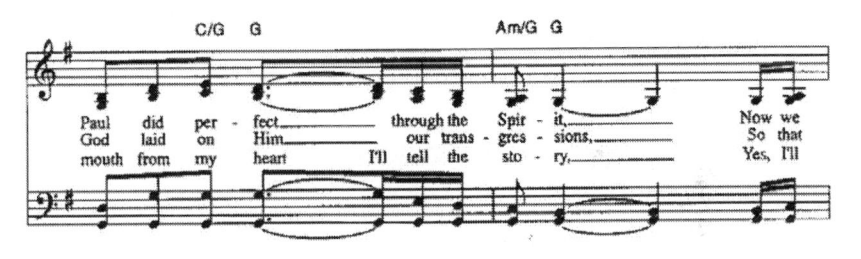

1. Jer-e-mi-ah of old spoke a-bout it; "The good way" he called it, which he too strode. The same Paul did per-fect through the Spir-it, Now we call it "That Old Ro-mans Road."
2. Way-stops here tell of sin and sal-va-tion, That our Lord died for us on Cal-va-ry, That our God laid on Him our trans-gres-sions, So that we might walk here in vic-to-ry!
3. Chap-ter ten says we must give Him glo-ry, And con-fess He a-rose from death and shame. With my mouth from my heart I'll tell the sto-ry, Yes, I'll shout it, "Christ is Lord!" Praise His name!

That Old Romans Road - 2

REFRAIN

I thank God for "That Old Romans Road," For, praise God, on that road Christ set me free! And when there I gave Him my sin's load, In exchange He gave Heaven to me.

From that 'Hole' Up to Heaven

"...Look to the hole of the pit whence ye are digged." – Isaiah 51:1
"God...made us to sit together in heavenly places in Christ Jesus." – Ephesians 2:4, 6
Nothing can "separate us from the love of God...in Christ Jesus our Lord." – Rom. 8:38, 39

Words and Music by
John W. Evans

1. Of what in my past may this poor man extol? To what, looking back, can I proudly lay claim? Isaiah declares we're just dug from a past. Therefore looking back, I've no balm for my shame.

2. Yes, God in His word says in Christ grace is given, Which staggers my mind when I look at my past. But, more, now with Christ I am "seated in" Heav-en". Co-heir with Him there to His Heaven so vast!

3. Dear Lord, knowing that I'm an heir to your Heaven, Though a sinner once dug from that "hole" by your grace, Please help me each day to reject all sin's leaven, So I'll not be ashamed when I look on your face!

© Copyright 2000 by John Evans, 7907 Jamaica Rd., North, Jacksonville, FL 32216. All rights reserved.

From that 'Hole' Up to Heaven - 2

REFRAIN

I have come a long way from that "hole" up to Heaven! In my standing in Christ I'm now one with Him there! And God's word too declares that more grace will be given, So in standing and state with Christ God's Heaven I'll share!

162

Thank God the Garbage Is Gone

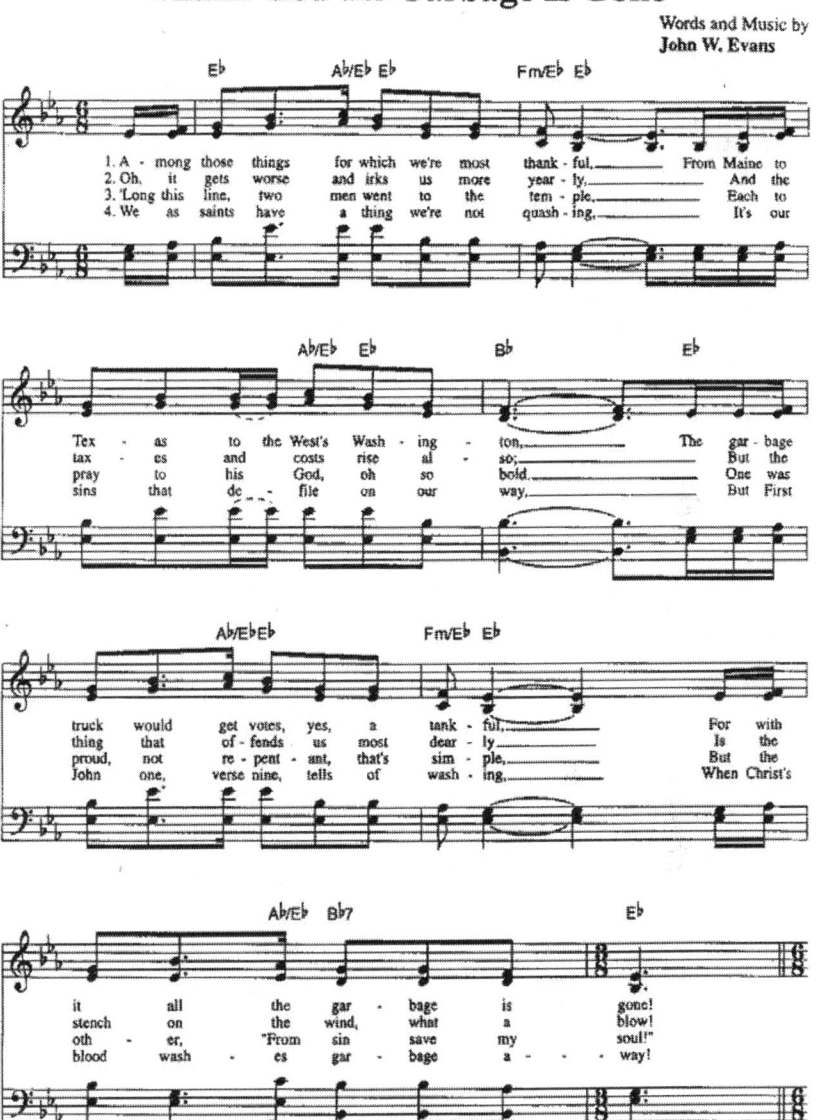

Words and Music by
John W. Evans

1. A-mong those things for which we're most thank-ful, From Maine to Tex-as to the West's Wash-ing-ton, The gar-bage truck would get votes, yes, a tank - ful. For with it all the gar-bage is gone!
2. Oh, it gets worse and irks us more year-ly, And the tax-es and costs rise al-so; But the thing that of-fends us most dear-ly, Is the stench on the wind, what a blow!
3. 'Long this line, two men went to the tem-ple, Each to pray to his God, oh so bold. One was proud, not re-pent-ant, that's sim-ple, But the oth-er, "From sin save my soul!"
4. We as saints have a thing we're not quash-ing, It's our sins that de-file on our way, But First John one, verse nine, tells of wash-ing, When Christ's blood wash-es gar-bage a-way!

© Copyright 2000 by John W. Evans, 7907 Jamaica Rd., North, Jacksonville, FL 32216. All rights reserved.

Thank God the Garbage Is Gone 2

REFRAIN

Oh, we thank God the garbage is gone! Yes, we thank God the garbage is gone! Well, it's reeked far too long, But we now sing this song, Oh, we thank God the garbage is gone.

164

What a Day!

Words and Music by
John W. Evans

1. What a day! What a day! What a day! O, what a day! When my Je- sus washed my sins all a- way! What a day! What a day! Now I'm hap-py on the King's High- way! What a day! What a day! O, what a day! 2. Hal- le- lu- jah! Hal- le- lu! Hal- le- lu- jah! Hal- le- lu! Hey, a-

© Copyright 2000 by John W. Evans, 7907 Jamaica Road, North, Jacksonville, FL. 32216. All rights reserved.

C C/E A♭7/E♭ G7/D G7
head my Heav - 'nly home is in view! Hal - le -
C C7 F C F7
lu - jah! Hal - le - lu! Say, there's room on this road for you! Hal - le -
C F C/G G7 C C/B♭ A7
lu - jah! Hal - le - lu - jah! Hal - le - lu! 3. Praise the
D D7 G D A7
Lord! Praise the Lord! Praise the Lord! O, praise the Lord! How
D D/F♯ B♭7/F A7/E A7
great to walk with God in sweet ac - cord! Praise the

What a Day! - 3

You're Worth a World of Little Sparrows

Luke 21:2,3; Matthew 10:29, 31; John 11

Words and Music by
John W. Evans

1. Our Lord Jesus stood beside the Treasury, And saw the widow giving there to God's cause; He knew she gave her two mites out of poverty, And I
2. The two sisters of the town of Bethany, With Laz'rus dead thought his Friend didn't care. But when He came and saw there all their misery, He also
3. And so today in a world of awesome needs, We as mortals should still seek this Friend. Yes, I urge you call on Christ for His super deeds, That He still

© Copyright 2000 John W. Evans, 7907 Jamaica Rd., N.
Jacksonville, FL 32216. All rights reserved.

know forever blessed that widow was.
saw their simple faith expressed in prayer.
cares for needy souls you can depend.

REFRAIN
For He's the widow's as-sis-tor And the poor man's up-lift-er, Though your hopes and your dreams have grown dim. He sees the little sparrow fall, And He'll surely hear your call, You're worth a world of little sparrows to Him!

Deeper, Let's Go Deeper

"...Here is water; what hinders me to be baptized?" – Acts 8:36b
"Are ye able to be baptized with the baptism that I am baptized with?" – Matt. 20:22

Words and Music by
John W. Evans

1. I had trusted in the Lord for my salvation, And baptism in the river lay ahead; But the preacher in the stream showed hesitation, To proceed into deep waters, then I said:
2. My baptizer must have had some fear of water, For from waist-high depths he surely showed he shied; Yes, he paused out there in still too shallow water; That's when proclaiming a bit louder that I cried:
3. Well, at last we got in to the deeper waters, More like the depths of love that I had for my God. Some are not concerned at all for going deeper, And some with God will cross "this river" feet dry-shod!
4. Our Lord Jesus came to die in a "baptism," A descent into dire judgment for our sins; And before the deepest waters of that mission, He was prepared our souls to save, so entered in!

© Copyright 2000 by John W. Evans, 7907 Jamaica Rd., N., Jacksonville, FL 32216. All rights reserved.

REFRAIN
G7 C G7
Oh, let's wade in - to deep wa - ters for bap - ti - sm, Ev - er
C G G7 C
in - to deep - er wa - ters with our God; Our bap - ti - sm like our love should go still
C F/C C G7 C
deep - er. For on - ly depths of deep de - vo - tion He ap - plauds.

God's Lamb as Lion King Shall Reign!

Genesis 49:9a; John 1:29; Revelation 5:5b (Williams Tr.)

Words and Music by
John W. Evans

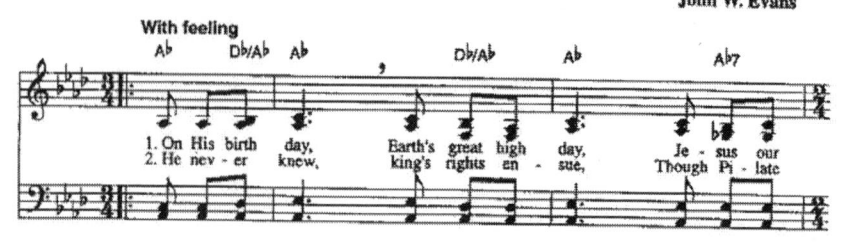

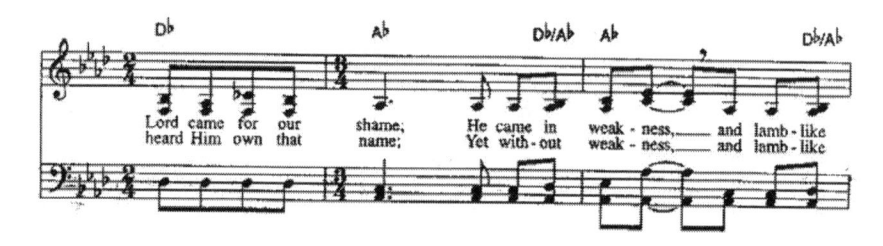

1. On His birth day, Earth's great high day, Je-sus our Lord came for our shame; He came in weak-ness, and lamb-like meek-ness, The "Lamb of God" John named His name. I nev-er saw Him, so nev-er knew Him, When as that low-ly Lamb He

2. He nev-er knew, king's rights en-sue, Though Pi-late heard Him own that name; Yet with-out weak-ness and lamb-like meek-ness, He rose from death in val-id claim! God help me nev-er, as cow-ard ev-er De-ny this Lamb for sin-ners

© Copyright 2000 by John W. Evans, 7907 Jamaica Rd., North, Jacksonville, FL 32216. All rights reserved.

God's Lamb as Lion King Shall Reign - 2

came. Born in a manger, to men a stranger. I never
slain. Though foes assail me, Lord, help me daily De-clare He'll

saw Him die for my blame! But, Oh, I'll see Him! Praise God I'll
come as King to reign! *(2nd time)* Oh, yes, I'll

see Him, When with great pow'r He comes again! Then without

weakness, and lamb-like meekness, God's con-q'ring Lamb as King shall

reign! I'll laud once more, Whom I adore, That "lowly

God's Lamb as Lion King Shall Reign! - 3

My Hallelujah Home

*Inspired, in part, by Robert Frost's "Death of a Hired Man,"
But mostly by the message of the Bible on Heaven*

Words and Music by
John Evans

1. Oh, the po-et has said of the place that we call home. When the ways of the world have worn thin, That when you knock at the door, Be you ev-er so poor, Well, the doors to o-pen wide,
2. Here you may have a home, and it's be-yond com-pare, With all the com-forts of life there in view, But now tell me, dear friend, When you come to life's end, Then Do you too
3. Oh do make sure you have up in Heav-en that home. When the ways of this world have worn thin, Give your heart to Christ who died, Heav-en's with

© Copyright 2000 by John Evans, 7907 Jamaica Road, N. Jacksonville, FL 32216.
All rights reserved.

My Hallelujah Home - 2

folks there just have to take you in.
have a home in Heav'n there for you?
Hal-le-lu-jahs you'll en-ter in.

Refrain
But in Heav'n I have a home with the warm-est wel-come there, It's not a
Oh, in Heav'n

"have to" but a "glad to" home, you see! Bought by the

blood of God's dear Son, Who'll meet me there when day is

done, My Hal-le-lu-jah Home in Heav'n waits for me!

My Hallelujah Home - 3

My Hal - le - lu - jah Home in Heav'n waits for me!

My Hal - le - lu - jah Home in Heav'n waits for me!

Bought by the blood of God's dear Son, Who'll meet me there when day is

done, My Hal - le - lu - jah Home in Heav'n waits for me.

Released with Great Joy I'll Go Home

*For those Christians terminally ill who don't wish for more life supports,
but really want to go home to be with Jesus*

Words and Music by
John W. Evans

1. When I come to the end of life's jour-ney, And a high-er road beck-ons to me, I would not have sad tears with my go-ing, For re-leased I'll be glo-rious-ly free.
2. Yes, I know we are sched-uled for judg-ment, And as sin-less I nev-er claimed to be, But God for the Lamb slain at Cal-v'ry, Where God's jus-tice met mer-cy for me.
3. Please don't ask for me more time, dear loved ones, For life sup-ports for my suf-f'rings a-head; For, I see my Lord's face in the sun-set, And its love-glow is Cal-va-ry red.

© Copyright 2000 by John W. Evans, 7907 Jamaica Road, North,
Jacksonville, FL 32216. All rights reserved.

Released with Great Joy I'll Go Home - 2

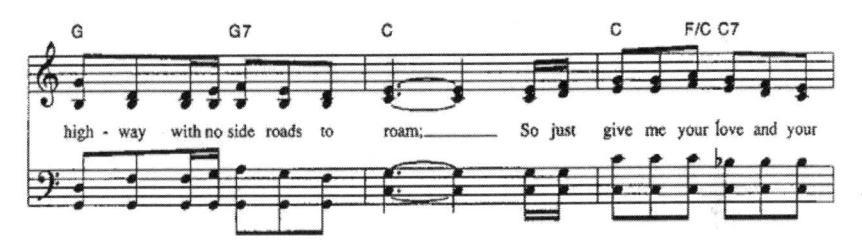

REFRAIN

Oh, I long to be-gin on this jour-ney,_____ On this high-way with no side roads to roam;____ So just give me your love and your God-speed,____ Then re-leased with great joy I'll go home.____

Made in the USA
San Bernardino, CA
27 June 2015